The Digital Shift and Social Research

Methods and Practices

Paolo Diana

University of Salerno

Critical Perspectives on Social Science

VERNON PRESS

www.vernonpress.com

In the Americas:
Vernon Press
1000 N West Street, Suite 1200,
Wilmington, Delaware 19801
United States

In the rest of the world:
Vernon Press
C/Sancti Espiritu 17,
Malaga, 29006
Spain

Critical Perspectives on Social Science

Library of Congress Control Number: 2025940199

Digital Object Identifier (DOI): 10.54094/b-413fa9ac28

ISBN: 979-8-8819-0354-1

Also available: 979-8-8819-0077-9 [Hardback]; 979-8-8819-0363-3 [PDF, E-Book]

Cover design by Vernon Press with elements by macrovector_official on Freepik.

Table of Contents

List of Figures

List of Tables

Author Biography

Paolo Diana is a full professor at the Department of Human, Philosophical and Educational Sciences (DISUFF) at the University of Salerno in Italy, where he teaches Sociology, Research methods (qualitative and quantitative), Data analysis, Digital methods, Sociology of sport and well-being and Sociology of health. He holds a PhD from the Department of Sociology of the University of Salerno, and he has participated in several European projects about adult and juvenile prisoners.

Paolo Diana's areas of expertise include quantitative and qualitative research methods and data analysis. He explores new frontiers in social research, including digital methods, mixed methods, open data analysis, and complexity. His work includes topics such as immigration, deviance, youth, southern Italy and its representations, juvenile delinquency, social issues, sport, and media. He is particularly interested in the practice of teaching research methods, focusing on the relationship between new technologies and learning, e-learning, smart learning, ICT, and digital knowledge. He is also involved in the monitoring and evaluation of international and EU projects.

He has published numerous articles in academic journals and has been recognised for his excellence in research, undergraduate, and postgraduate teaching and outreach.

Foreword

The following work is the result of years of study, observation, and research that I conducted as part of the Social Research Methods course at the University of Salerno in southern Italy. This endeavour presented me with a unique opportunity to study the behaviour and needs of my students in relation to the teaching and learning of social research methods. I focused on the acquisition of theoretical knowledge, methodological practices, and fieldwork within undergraduate and postgraduate programs in sociology and social research.

During these years, I have witnessed significant changes and developments in the field of social research methodology. This experience has enabled me to adapt and refine my teaching strategies to better meet the changing demands of the academic environment and the different learning styles of my students. The lessons learnt have significantly shaped the content and approach of this book.

Over the years, I have had the privilege of publishing numerous contributions on these topics together with my close collaborators Maria Carmela Catone and Giovannipaolo Ferrari, whom I hereby thank for their invaluable co-operation. Our joint endeavours have enriched my understanding and contributed significantly to the depth and breadth of this work. This book is inspired by and builds on the numerous papers and articles we have published over the years, all of which are cited in this book. It is intended to summarize and synthesize our joint research and findings.

Compiling this work has been both challenging and enriching. It reflects not only my personal academic journey but also the collective experiences of my students and colleagues who have been involved in this endeavour. Their feedback, questions, and engagement have been a constant source of motivation and inspiration.

Finally, I would like to thank the students of the courses and workshops on Digital Methods for Social Research at the University of Salerno for kindly allowing the use of the images and elaborations from their final group projects.

I hope that this book will serve as a valuable resource for students, teachers, and researchers alike, providing them with a comprehensive understanding of social research methods and their practical applications. I firmly believe that, through continued exploration and discussion, we can advance the field of social research and contribute to the development of more effective and impactful methods.

Salerno, 7 June 2024
Paolo Diana

Introduction

This volume, titled *The Digital Shift and Social Research Methods and Practices*, is the result of theoretical reflections and empirical research carried out in recent years on distance learning in universities and the provision of courses on social research methodology. The following work is the result of years of study, observation, and research that I carried out as part of the Social Research Methods courses at the University of Salerno in southern Italy. This book is intended for a diverse audience involved in social research and education. It primarily addresses university lecturers, academic researchers, and doctoral students in the social sciences who are interested in methodological innovation and the integration of digital tools in research design and analysis. At the same time, it is also aimed at higher education instructors, pedagogical trainers, and curriculum designers, especially those engaged in teaching research methods or developing blended and online learning environments. While academics may be more interested in theoretical and epistemological debates, educators and trainers will find practical insights, case studies, and didactic strategies useful for planning and delivering social research courses. The book is designed to bridge the gap between methodological reflection and pedagogical application, offering content that is both conceptually rigorous and grounded in classroom experience.

I wanted to take the opportunity to study and explore the behaviour and needs of my students in relation to the teaching and learning of social research methods and the acquisition of theoretical knowledge, methodological practices, and fieldwork within undergraduate and postgraduate courses in sociology and social research. Our efforts to systematically organise our observations and findings coincided with the exceptional situation of the COVID-19 pandemic affecting our academic system (Diana, Ferrari and Dommarco, 2021).

The ubiquitous presence of digital technology has revolutionized daily life, often accompanied by unbridled optimism about its impact. However, the pandemic has also revealed fractures in the relationship between the use of digital technologies and academic education. This book addresses the teaching of social research methodology in academia, focusing on didactic innovations. This requires a transversal view that considers the specificities of the discipline, including theoretical and linguistic issues, methodological approaches, and technical applications. The vast amount of unstructured information available through digital technologies opens new possibilities for the study of contemporary society and requires a rethinking of the traditional empirical apparatus.

The first key component of this change relates to the characteristics of the discipline, addressing both traditional and new theoretical issues, methodological approaches, and technical applications. The second component relates to understanding the needs, practices, languages, and identities of students. This includes promoting students' active participation in environments that facilitate the exchange and effective use of technological tools. Paolo Ferri (2011) describes the new generations' approach to knowledge as "open source," "collaborative," and "multitasking," i.e., working on several cognitive tasks at the same time.

University teachers must carefully select teaching tools and resources, considering accessibility, real and virtual spaces and the digital devices available to students. Considering which pedagogical approach is best suited to support student learning is crucial and is closely related to the technological components. This volume explores the strengths and weaknesses of these approaches, focusing on the design, implementation, and delivery of social research methods.

The first chapter looks at social research methodology, learning, teaching, and the new frontiers of the discipline arising from digital developments. It provides an in-depth analysis of how the proliferation of digital tools and platforms has expanded the methods available to researchers. This chapter examines the theoretical shifts necessary for the integration of digital tools into social research and explores how digital environments influence human behaviour, social interactions, and cultural norms. It also looks at the ethical considerations that arise when using digital tools for research and emphasizes the need for researchers to rethink the basic premises of their work.

The second chapter explores how digital tools can be used to increase learner engagement and promote collaborative learning experiences. It looks at strategies for promoting engagement using digital tools, creating collaborative learning environments through digital interfaces and redefining assessment practices in digital learning contexts. This chapter emphasizes the importance of using digital tools not only to engage students but also to facilitate meaningful interactions and collaborations among them, enhancing the overall learning experience.

Empirical studies carried out over the years in the social research methodology courses at the University of Salerno in Italy are an essential part of this book. In the last three chapters, these studies and their results are presented in detail to illustrate how pedagogical practices can be renewed in the teaching of research methods and how teaching methods can be evaluated simultaneously in a critical and reflective perspective, considering the possibilities offered by digital resources. These experiences include courses such as Social Research

Methodology and Open Data[1] for Social Research, as well as the Digital Methods for Social Research course. These studies demonstrate how the integration of digital resources can provide new opportunities for research practice and teaching that allow for critical reflection and greater adaptability of teaching methods. These studies contribute to creating an intergenerational educational pact that teaches new forms of communication and interaction between students and teachers that are central to reshaping teaching and learning in the digital age.

With the advent of digital technology, the landscape of social research has changed considerably. It is in this context that we present the fourth chapter: "Narratives in social research: Tradition and innovation," which explores the evolving role of narrative methods in sociological analysis. This chapter highlights the interplay between traditional and emerging narrative techniques and emphasizes the impact of digital technology on empirical research. The integration of digital narratives opens new ways of understanding complex social phenomena and expands the scope and depth of qualitative research.

In addition, this book addresses the profound transformation of social research methods through digital technology. The digital transformation in social research requires researchers to rethink fundamental premises and adapt to digital environments that influence behaviour, ethical considerations, interactions, and norms. The book addresses the theoretical and methodological challenges, engagement and collaboration, ethical considerations, and pedagogical challenges of teaching digital social research methods. The findings from this book are intended to inspire innovative approaches to research and deepen understanding of the intricate relationship between technology and social science. This exploration illuminates the complexities and possibilities of social research in the digital age and provides a comprehensive resource for social science students, educators, and practitioners.

---

[1] Open Data refers to data that is freely available and can be used, modified, and shared by anyone without legal, technical, or financial restrictions. The data is usually published in a machine-readable format to facilitate access and use. Open data initiatives aim to promote transparency, innovation, and collaboration in various areas such as government, education, research, and business. By making data accessible, open data encourages the creation of new knowledge, services, and applications that benefit society (Ruijer et al., 2020; Cazzanti, 2016).

Chapter 1
Theoretical and methodological challenges in digital social research

1.1 Adapting research methodology to the digital age: Student attitudes and approaches

Although undergraduate and postgraduate university teaching may appear to non-specialists to be a simple, repetitive and automatic task, it is actually a highly complex activity (Ferreira and Serpa, 2017). The creation and delivery of a successful academic learning pathway typically involves a wide range of actors (professors, tutors, managers, etc.), who must navigate the multitude of ever-changing macro and micro factors, including human, pedagogical, psychological, technological, socio-cultural, and economic. In recent decades, technological change and the various demands of social, economic, and political stakeholders have led to many teaching and learning shifts in higher education. Universities must increasingly focus on aligning teaching performance with research performance and must demonstrate that they are able to provide quality education that can prepare students for a professional future (Ferreira and Serpa, 2017). Furthermore, as part of broader processes of standardization and the datafication[1] of contemporary academic systems (Hanson, 2005; Jarke and Breiter, 2019; Williamson, Bayne and Shay, 2020), which are primarily focused on measuring and monitoring outcomes, the need has emerged to apply forms of sociological imagination to teaching practices (Halasz and Kaufman, 2008) and the context in which they take place (Hanson, 2005) in order to promote the social, relational, and intellectual components that underpin the work of education (Harley and Natalier, 2013). Based on this broader context, the content and structure of a college course obligate the instructor to carefully plan an educational pathway in which the knowledge content of the discipline is accompanied by in-depth reflection on various characteristics to ensure the success of higher education.

---

[1] Datafication refers to the process of transforming various aspects of life, activities, and information into data that can be quantified and analysed. Social actions, interactions, behaviours, and even thoughts are transformed into digital data that can be collected, processed, and used for analysis, decision-making, and other purposes. Datafication enables the detailed tracking and understanding of phenomena that were previously difficult to measure, fuelling insights and innovation in various fields.

As far as the field of social sciences is concerned, the teaching of sociological disciplines in higher education poses its own challenge due to the peculiarities of these subjects, which require a heuristic interdisciplinarity. It is crucial to foster critical and reflective thinking (Ferreira and Serpa, 2017) at multiple levels through a process of "exploration, excitement, and respect" (Harley and Natalier, 2013, p. 394) and to cultivate a dynamic relationship between learners and the world, rather than simply asking students to identify with an external disciplinary object full of content (Harley and Natalier, 2013).

More specifically, teaching sociological disciplines is about providing learners with the appropriate knowledge and skills to distinguish scientific knowledge from common sense and to propose alternative images of society based on methodological rigor. It is thus about encouraging students to adopt learning paths that allow them to investigate and interpret social reality by adopting a non-obvious point of view (Collins, 1992) and finding and highlighting the less obvious aspects of social phenomena (Stefanizzi, 2012). During an undergraduate course in the social sciences, students are guided to develop a broad range of sociological skills necessary to grasp and interpret the complexity of phenomena that characterize contemporary society: theoretical (knowledge and development of sociological categories); methodological (knowledge, production, selection of appropriate methods, and techniques to collect, analyse and interpret information); linguistic (development and rigorous application of a scientific vocabulary); technical (application of technical, strategic, organizational measures); social (relationships within the scientific community and with other actors); communicative (exchange of ideas with different actors); ethical (understanding and adherence to the researcher's code of conduct); etc. (Ni, 2013, p. 209; Ferreira and Serpa, 2017, p. 5).

A fundamental component of a higher education social science program, and particularly a sociology curriculum, is the broad area of research methodology, which covers various scientific topics, such as the general principles of science, the ontological and epistemological elements of knowledge that underlie scientific paradigms, as well as qualitative and quantitative approaches and techniques. In general, research methodology plays an important role in sociological education as it enables learners to understand the relationships between the subject matter of the sociological discipline and its formal structures. In addition, it promotes an understanding of the scientific value of sociology as an empirical science, characterized using procedures that combine theoretical-conceptual aspects with those that are operational, experimental, and observational (Memoli, 2009). The awareness of the regulative structures that contribute to making sociology a scientific discipline and the analysis of the correctness and appropriateness of the methods used in the field of study

(Stefanizzi, 2012) are therefore part of the methodological training provided during the academic learning path.

The complex nature of the methodological discipline, linked to both theoretical and technical concepts, raises several issues at the college level from a pedagogical point of view, forcing the professor to adopt appropriate ways to provide students with a wide range of knowledge and skills. Typically, scholarly studies focus mainly on the development and application of methods and techniques for conducting empirical research in the social sciences and instead neglect fundamental aspects required for *teaching* the subject at the college level, such as course design, delivery, and assessment (Wagner, Garner and Kawulich, 2011). According to several studies (Wagner, Garner and Kawulich, 2011; Kilburn, Nind and Wiles, 2014; Earley, 2014), the teaching of research methods lacks a systematic pedagogical culture and, unlike other disciplines, is not an established area of scholarship. As a result, teachers of social research methods typically "rely on a network of peers, scattered research literature, and much trial and error" (Earley, 2014, p. 243), as there is no recognized research literature on teaching methods (Earley, 2014). The studies that have been published on this topic tend to be small or very specific and based on a particular teaching experience (Nind, Kilburn and Luff, 2015; Lewthwaite and Holmes, 2018).

Despite this lack of systematic discussion about the teaching of research methodology, some sociologists have over time raised questions about the characteristics of the discipline, its role in sociology curricula, and the relationship between research and teaching in this academic field. Burgess (1990), for example, in an article entitled *Objectives in teaching and using research methodology*, examined the place and function of research methodology in college sociology curricula, highlighting some crucial unanswered questions, such as the status of methodology and what it should include in sociological research training; in this context, other scholars have raised the question of whether formal methodology teaching should be integrated with the study of problems in content areas (Brown, 1979). Other related issues have concerned the acquisition of methodological skills by sociology students in terms of research skills and competence. Bulmer and Burgess (1981) stated on this issue that the overall aim is to produce sociologists who understand methodological issues. Another point they raised related to the skills of the professor who teaches social research methods; here they posed some open questions such as "Who should be involved in teaching research methodology? Should this be the job of a specialized methodologist? Should it be taught by all sociologists?" (Bulmer and Burgess, 1981, p. 587).

In light of these considerations, the academic community has recently begun to address the multiple challenges underlying the teaching and learning of social research methods in sociology education and to advocate for the development of a pedagogical culture of methodological learning in the social sciences. An interest in improving social science research education (Nind and Lewthwaite, 2020) is also evident among policymakers (Nind and Lewthwaite, 2020) and several institutions, particularly in the UK, that have begun to invest in training in social (mainly quantitative) research methods. Q-step, for example, a £19.5 million program launched in 2013/14 by the Nuffield Foundation, the Economic and Social Research Council and the Higher Education Funding Council for England, aims to significantly improve education and training in the quantitative social sciences in the UK. The National Centre for Research Methods (NCRM), established in 2004 as part of the Economic and Social Research Council, focuses on delivering projects, training, and events and providing resources to improve the quality and range of methodological approaches and techniques. To this end, the NCRM has developed "the pedagogy of methodological learning" (Nind and Lewthwaite, 2020), a research project designed to promote and support pedagogical development in the teaching of social research methods by examining and analysing case studies of methodological and pedagogical innovations drawn from the learning and teaching experiences of researchers and social methodology experts (Nind et al., 2019; Nind and Lewthwaite, 2020). Specifically, Melanie Nind and Sarah Lewthwaite (2020) have developed a conceptual-empirical typology of pedagogy for teaching social science research methods using a mix of qualitative methods involving both teachers and students and based on the categories of approach, strategy, tactics, and tasks. This has helped to introduce a dynamic tool for developing good practice in the teaching of social science research methods.

Other recent studies on the teaching of the discipline have examined various interrelated components, including the practices, approaches, tools, and resources used by professors, as well as the experiences, difficulties, skills, and attitudes of students, and finally, the dialogue that results from the interdependence between students and instructors. Much of the research focuses on how to cultivate the effective teaching of social research methods and promote learning of the discipline among both students and early career professionals in a variety of contexts to enrich their research experience.

Most contemporary work advocates student-centred learning methods (Barraket, 2005) and experiential forms of learning-by-doing processes that focus on both students' cognitive and social skills and limitations (Gobo, 2009) to facilitate research practice (Atkinson and Hunt, 2008; Aguado, 2009). According to these approaches, current teaching models in many countries should be revised to attract students' attention and stimulate their interest in subjects such as social research methods, which do not attract interest as easily as other, more substantial subjects (Gobo, 2009). From this perspective, in addition to developing conceptual knowledge, it is important that learners know that methods imply forms of practices that need to be evaluated in their relation to the world (Abbott, 2004, p. 11).

Although more recent pedagogical approaches have followed this school of thinking, the role of research practice as a fundamental component of teaching social research methodology was addressed as early as the 1980s. Wakeford (1981), for example, argued for a workshop approach to engaging students in research projects and providing them with opportunities to learn about research practice, linking the different stages and selecting and applying techniques that relate to particular cognitive goals, problems and theories.

Moreover, many scholars have argued that the experience of research practice should be as 'real' as possible (e.g., Burgess and Bulmer, 1981; Halfpenny, 1981; Burgess, 1990; Pfeffer and Rogalin, 2012; Lewthwaite and Nind, 2016, etc.) to foster soft skills such as perseverance, imagination, creative craft and engagement. At the same time, the practice of research is not a matter of ad-hoc decision-making (Hammersley, 2012). It is not simply the automatic execution of more operational tasks, but encompasses all the intertwined stages, from theory formation and conceptualization to the technical and ethical concerns associated with conducting sociological research. This is because the research process involves more than the mere application of a particular set of techniques in a particular context and is characterized by a reciprocal combination of "the conceptual and the empirical worlds, of deduction and induction, taking place simultaneously" (Bechhofer, 1974, p. 73).

Looking at recent studies, Lewthwaite and Nind (2016) created a roundtable discussion with international social research experts who noted that there is a need to engage learners in the practice of research and make it 'visible' by drawing on examples from real contexts so that learners can understand otherwise abstract categories and concepts (Keenan and Fontaine, 2012). Pfeffer and Rogalin (2012) conducted a brief case study in which they identified possible teaching strategies that involve conducting real-world research through active learning tasks and discussion-based learning. Trowler (2005) and Tarifa and Zhupa (2014) also advocate teaching sociological theory with an empirical orientation to enhance students' abilities to apply sociological theory to everyday contexts. In line with this vision, Kilburn, Nind and Wiles (2014) suggest engaging learners in problem-based activities where they can practice, experiment and engage with a topical issue. According to Adriaensen, Kerremans and Slootmaeckers (2015, p. 2), "methods are not motor skills but require constant adaptation to the research question and the research context." For this reason, the use of experiential learning, based on students' experiences with the subjects of the field, allows them to learn from their mistakes and acquire skills through iterations of trial and error (Adriaensen et al., 2015, p. 2).

Atkinson and Hunt (2008) described a workshop experience based on inquiry-led learning. This is based on the idea that students should think and act like sociologists by engaging in an active process of inquiry, dynamic questioning, and the construction of sociological knowledge. In contrast, Lovekamp, Soboroff and Gillespie (2017) have developed a collaborative task based on the completion of some quantitative research tasks that promotes critical thinking, comparative analysis, self-reflection, and statistical literacy.

Another example of how to engage students' interest is to give them the experience of planning a research project, i.e. introduce an activity that enables learners to link research methods to a substantive issue (Cutler, 1987), gain an understanding of the different stages of research and enable them to work in a specific context (Burgess, 1981), as they need to

> grapple with research design, gain access to research, deal with field relationships, relate research problems and research methods, and develop links between theory and research (Burgess, 1981, p. 492).

At the same time, these types of activities require a significant amount of time and commitment from both professors and students and do not seem to be appropriate or easy to accomplish with large numbers of students. Research by Sandra Winn (1995) describes both the benefits of a social research methods course in which students participate in a real research project funded by an external client and the ways in which some of the difficulties that can be encountered in this type of learning can be overcome, pointing to the value that this form of learning strategy brings.

Other emerging research also relates to the role and identity of social research methods professors, recognizing that the development of a professional academic identity in research methodology is an essential factor in supporting a community of practice and promoting the advancement of the discipline (Daniel, 2018a). On this topic, Daniel (2018a) conducted an empirical analysis with 144 academics from 139 universities in nine countries who taught research methodology to find out how they built their professional academic identity in research methodology. The main result showed that the teaching of research methods at college level exists in multiple forms: These forms arise from the wide diversity of academics with different backgrounds and experiences, some of whom feel they are experienced researchers, while others associate themselves with a particular research method and follow a particular ontological and epistemological view.

Recent developments also emphasize the use of digital technologies in the teaching of social research methods. For example, one learning experience that aims to increase student engagement in research is the implementation of gamified activities (Sillaots, 2014; Zuckerman et al., 2015; Mattar, Souza and de

Oliveira Beduschi, 2017; Snelson et al., 2017). For example, Zuckerman et al. (2015) have developed a mobile platform for scientific inquiry called Ruzo, which allows learners to develop research projects as customized mobile apps. This platform allows learners to collect and visualize data using a web-based interactive tool and gives them the opportunity to go through all phases of empirical research. In addition, further theoretical studies and experiences with the design and implementation of a wide range of online teaching have been carried out in recent years. In particular, professors of sociological disciplines and social research methods are beginning to reflect on the strengths and weaknesses of e-learning systems when it comes to supporting and inspiring sociology students in their learning (King, 2015; El-Najjar, 2018; Snelson, 2019). For example, Rock et al. (2016) suggested practical examples of e-learning activities based on virtual world simulations to engage social science students and help them understand concepts of multivariate analysis; Thompson, Leonard and Bridier (2019) explored the use of online discussion forums to reduce anxiety about statistics. The teaching experiences and research I have conducted over the years also follow this trend, focusing on how disciplinary change and innovation in research methodology at the teaching level can be supported by specific e-learning pathways (Arcangeli and Diana, 2009; Diana and Catone, 2016; 2018; Catone and Diana, 2017; 2019a; 2019c).

Furthermore, the need to investigate the functioning and value of e-learning in higher education teaching, and in this case specifically in the field of social research methodology, becomes even more pressing when considering the general changes currently observed in the context of the spread of the recent COVID-19 virus (Diana, Ferrari and Dommarco, 2021). The recent pandemic has led to broader forms of dematerialization of teaching and learning processes, forcing college teachers to rethink their 'modus operandi' in terms of content, tools and relationships with students (Gillis and Krull, 2020). As for the impact of the pandemic on the teaching of social research methods, some opportunities for discussion are beginning to open, such as the online workshop hosted by *Sociological Review* on July 20, 2020, where the possibilities and problems of teaching research methods in this time of crisis were discussed by social research methods lecturers from many universities around the world.

Other outstanding issues in the teaching of social research methods concern the evolution of the discipline resulting from the development of information and communication technology and the growing amount of data generated by software, apps, people, digital devices, etc., a development that challenges social research to a profound reflection on the epistemological, methodological, and technical apparatus that characterizes social research. This innovation also affects the didactic dimension of the discipline, requiring methodology professors to redesign research methodology programs to provide students with a critical understanding of the challenges and complexities of collecting, analysing, and interpreting such large amounts of data (Daniel, 2018b).

Finally, considerable recent research was included and summarized in literature reviews, most of which indicated that the teaching of social research methods occupies a marginal position (Kilburn, Nind and Wiles, 2014), despite the recent growing interest in this topic. An initial systematic review of the available literature by Wagner, Garner and Kawulich (2011) based on 195 articles published between 1997 and 2007 revealed seven main themes related to the teaching of research methods: teaching research methods in general from a theoretical perspective, teaching qualitative topics with a focus on data analysis, teaching quantitative research methods, teaching mixed quantitative and qualitative methods, specific techniques for teaching research methods, a pedagogical approach to research methods within a particular discipline, and teaching ethics in research. In their conclusions, the authors of the study also identified three major gaps that require comprehensive theoretical and empirical treatment:

> the role and characteristics of the teacher; the challenges of teaching and learning specific aspects of research methods; common similarities and differences in research methods across disciplines (Wagner, Garner and Kawulich, 2011, p. 82).

In 2014, Earley presented a review of 89 articles published between 1987 and 2012 to examine trends in research on the teaching and learning of research methods. From this review, the following themes emerged: the characteristics of students taking a research methods course in terms of their skills and attitudes towards the subject; the teaching methods and techniques, i.e., the pedagogical approach and strategies used in the courses; the content and learning objectives of a research methods course. In addition, this analysis also suggested that the development of a social research methods pedagogy should promote active learning approaches to teaching the course so that it provides "hands-on experiences with research methods" (Earley, 2014, p. 248).

Further research was conducted by Kilburn, Nind and Wiles (2014). They produced a thematic qualitative analysis of 24 published articles from 2007 to 2014 on the strategies planned and used by faculty to support the learning of research methods skills and abilities by undergraduate, postgraduate, and early career researchers in a range of contexts. The findings suggest three major pedagogical streams: making research visible, experiential learning, and reflection on the research process.

Other themes were explored by Sarah Lewthwaite and Michelle M. Holmes (2018), who analysed 30 leading social science research methods textbooks for postgraduate students and researchers to advance understanding of how methods textbooks help inform the teaching and learning of methods in higher education; to discover implicit and explicit pedagogy in methods textbook authorship; and to identify commonalities and differences in the pedagogy that plays a role in methods textbooks. Their findings show that these textbooks often play a crucial role in shaping the curriculum and pedagogical approaches in higher education. They found that there is a range of pedagogical strategies, some of which are explicit, while others are more implicit. The textbooks differ in their approach to integrating theoretical and practical aspects of social science research, and there are notable differences in the way they address the needs of postgraduate students compared to more experienced researchers. Furthermore, the study has shown the importance of textbooks not only for the transfer of methodological knowledge but also for students' understanding of the research process and the role of the researcher (Lewthwaite and Holmes, 2018).

1.2 Students' attitudes towards the study of research methodology

There is a growing body of literature on how social science students in higher education experience different difficulties when approaching social research methodology compared with those in other subjects (Crooks, Castleden and Van Meerveld, 2010; Braguglia and Jackson, 2012; Strangman and Knowles, 2012; Catone and Diana, 2016). A more comprehensive understanding of students' difficulties, attitudes, and perceptions of research methodology is needed to provide a solid foundation for the development of social research studies.

In examining the main problems encountered by students, an important aspect is the abstract nature that characterizes this methodological discipline. This makes it difficult for learners to translate conceptual knowledge into procedural knowledge, to apply familiar procedures to a new and different context, and to recognize the link between methodological content and practical research activities. Broers (2002) found a lack of problem-solving skills, even among students who had all the factual knowledge needed to complete the tasks. According to his research, understanding of abstract knowledge takes time to develop and be contextualized with more accessible ideas (Murtonen, 2015). Furthermore, due to the procedural component that underpins social research, there is a danger that research methodology "is seen less as a discipline and more as the acquisition of a set of isolated facts and skills without necessarily acquiring a deeper understanding of research" (Daniel, Kumar and Omar, 2018, p. 11). But as Hammersley (2012, p. 2) says, research methodology cannot be reduced to "a set of rules or techniques that can be taught and then applied". Even if the notion of a scientific method based on a set of rules that establish in advance an invariable sequence of instructions still prevails – as Marradi (1996) reminds us – the method is much more complex than a simple one-dimensional sequence of steps; the method can be understood as a path chosen by the researcher to guide his scientific activity step by step; the choice that accompanies all stages of the research process (from conceptualization to collection and analysis techniques to interpretation) makes empirical research "a cognitive process and not a simple process of validation of already formulated ideas" (Bailyn, 1977, p. 101).

Teaching methodology means activating critical thinking based on the idea that research does not mean being faithful to a single universal method but being sensitive to the specific needs of the problem and using forms of "creativity to transform formal procedures into practices capable of dealing with problematic situations that may arise during the research process" (Stefanizzi, 2012, p. 116). This is because the link between the epistemological, methodological, and technical levels is not rigid, but moves through interpretative approaches and practices that the researcher develops to support the coherence and value of their decisions (Stefanizzi, 2012).

In relation to the abstract nature of social research methods, another typical problem concerns the linguistic register, which plays a central role in this discipline, since methodology is also the argumentation or discourse about the method (Marradi, 2007) and it is within the methodological reflection that a scientific language is developed that is precise and free from ambiguity and vagueness.

According to many studies and experiences, social science students generally lack interest in learning research methods (Earley, 2014). They often do not recognize the value and importance of social research methods for understanding current social problems or for their daily lives to develop into engaged citizens (Payne and Williams, 2011). On the contrary, they tend to view this discipline as "boring, inaccessible and irrelevant" (Braguglia and Jackson, 2012, p. 348).

The level of difficulty learners face also changes depending on the types of methods and techniques covered in a course. With qualitative approaches, learners often tend to underestimate their value because they think they are softer or easier than quantitative research (Fontes and Piercy, 2000). Learners often believe that the research process in qualitative studies relies more on improvisation and personal skills than on strictly defined methodological procedures and therefore generally devote less time and concentration to studying these methods. As a result, they show large gaps in knowledge and application of the key principles that characterize the qualitative approach in their final exams (Catone and Diana, 2016).

With regard to quantitative methods, many studies have described the anxiety that social science students often feel (Papanastasiou, 2005; Papanastasiou and Zembylas, 2008; Williams et al., 2008; Payne and Williams, 2011). In a sociology course, the acquisition of the logical-statistical-mathematical aspects of quantitative social research contributes to the development of forms of thinking and critical argumentation that, along with other types of knowledge and skills, enable students to navigate the analysis and understanding of social phenomena. Activities such as counting, measuring, and calculating – typical of the quantitative method – do not only stem from technical skills, but rather imply logical reasoning systems that make it possible to carry out the different phases of designing empirical research, such as collecting information, analysing data, and interpreting results. Quantity, understood as

> the result of a measuring or counting process that indicates the intensity or frequency of a directly or indirectly observable phenomenon, cannot be reduced to a separate entity endowed with semantic autonomy and uncritically usable (Mingo, 2009, p. 21)

without being supported by argumentation activities. Instead, it requires a complex series of theoretical, logical, and operational phases that connect abstract concepts with their empirical correlates through a process of meaning-making: The meaning of quantities is therefore strictly dependent on the process by which they are generated and the contexts in which they are used (Mingo, 2009, p. 21). In this scenario, it is therefore fundamental that the student of a sociology course has the numerical skills to access, use, interpret, and communicate the quantitative information necessary to develop a conscious knowledge in the different contexts of today's world, which are increasingly interconnected and complex, to distinguish common sense from scientific reasoning and to analyse the knowledge of everyday life with methodological rigor.

Despite the crucial role that quantitative reasoning plays in analysing social phenomena, students generally face several biases and difficulties, which are particularly evident in the final exam. The main obstacles concern the different components of numerical reasoning, such as the adequate operational definition (classification, ordinality, cardinality) to be attributed to the type of properties (discrete, continuous), the basic arithmetic operations (counts, percentages, etc.), the interpretation and attribution of meaning to number and, finally, the ability to reflect and contextualize quantitative information (Catone and Diana, 2019a). The fear of quantitative methods among students has been described in many studies (Williams et al., 2008; 2016; Payne and Williams, 2011). Accordingly, the numeracy deficit identified in social science students is a combination of several aspects: first, a general prejudice towards the world of numbers, which are generally seen as abstract, difficult, distant, and detached from everyday life and the real world (Briggs at al., 2009); a false and distorted perception towards sociological studies, which are often seen as devoid of logical-statistical-mathematical content; certain culturally embedded prejudices based on the notion that mathematical and linguistic abilities are mutually exclusive and opposed (Murtonen and Lehtinen, 2003, p. 172); or the fact that

> some people view the world in terms of 'soft' and 'hard' issues or values, where hard issues are based on technical and numerical approaches and cannot be mastered by a person who behaves and thinks according to the soft approach (Murtonen and Lehtinen, 2003, p. 172);

or finally, a previous negative experience at school that has led to an aversion to dealing with numbers, helping to foster in some students the belief that they are 'not mathematical' and therefore incapable of mastering statistical concepts.

1.3 New frontiers of social research

Methodological training in the field of social research should take into account the evolution of the discipline, i.e., its changes and developments over time. In recent decades, the logic of scientific research in the social sciences has been enriched by innovations, in particular the advent of digital technologies, which have reopened long-standing questions on epistemological, methodological, and technical issues.

The first aspect to consider lies in the role that digital device, their ubiquity, and pervasiveness exert on many aspects of our lives, actively influencing, for example, our notions of self-understanding, social relations, practices, and institutions (Lupton, 2014). As Deborah Lupton argues,

> examining our interactions with digital technologies contributes to exploring the nature of human experience and also tells us much about the social world (Lupton, 2014, p. 2).

From this perspective, the internet is far from being seen as a second life. It is now deeply connected to our habits and is becoming a space where our opinions and practices evolve dynamically and influence our notions of identity. In this sense, the development of the digital world could be seen as a new kind of "total social fact" (Lury and Marres, 2015; Marres, 2017, p. 18).

Second, the process by which digital devices and technologies have become embedded in many aspects of our lives makes the web a living archive of information, traces, and data that offers new opportunities for understanding and analysing contemporary social issues (Marres, 2017). The world of work, electoral predictions, and socialization processes are all examples of typical phenomena that can be studied through the collection and analysis of data generated in digital contexts. In this scenario, it becomes clear that digital technologies represent a challenge that social scientists must face by taking into account the wealth of uses and meanings.

These dimensions are developed and explained by Nortje Marres (2017). She has provided a definition of this emerging field in the context of digital society research that assumes different but interrelated meanings by breaking it down into: (1) the topics of social research; (2) the methods of social research; (3) the platforms for engaging with audiences and publics of sociology (Diana and Ferrari, 2023; 2024; Marres, 2017).

The first concept considers the digital world as a phenomenon of contemporary society that affects many dimensions of social life, influencing our lifestyles, identities, relationships, etc.

The second vision of digital sociology is concerned with the methods and techniques of social research. In this context, Richard Rogers (2009) has made a distinction between 'natively digital' methods and the 'digitization' of existing methods. The former refers to the 'new' methods that are specifically tailored to the characteristics of digital devices[2]. The latter refers to existing empirical social research techniques that have been adapted and transformed for use in digital environments: web surveys and "*netnography*"[3], for example, are the digital equivalents of traditional survey and ethnographic techniques. Some forms of so-called digitized data objects also refer to secondary data provided by official statistical institutions and migrated to the Internet (Rogers, 2013). This distinction illustrates the complex and multi-layered configuration of the different research methods, which can be understood as a comprehensive combination of old and new techniques and methods.

---

[2] An example of "natively digital" methods, as described by Richard Rogers (2009), is the use of web scraping techniques to collect and analyse data from social media platforms. Unlike traditional methods, where existing surveys or interviews are digitised, native digital methods are designed to take advantage of the unique capabilities and structures of digital environments. Web scraping allows researchers to automatically extract large amounts of data from websites to analyse user-generated content, interaction patterns, and network structures specific to online platforms. This method capitalises on the digital nature of the data source and provides insights that are only accessible with digital tools and techniques.

[3] *Netnography*, a term coined by Robert Kozinets (1998), refers to a qualitative research methodology that adapts ethnographic research techniques to study communities and cultures that have emerged through computer-mediated communication. It is a systematic, interpretive study of online social interactions and digital communities that focuses on understanding the social practices, experiences, and behaviours of individuals in these virtual environments. *Netnography* is particularly useful for gaining insights into consumer behaviour, social media use, and other digital interactions, as it allows researchers to explore the rich, contextual details of online life.

Finally, the third concept underlying the study of digital society concerns the channels and tools that sociologists use to share their knowledge and engage with the public (Diana and Ferrari, 2023; 2024; Marres, 2017).

The meaning, uses, and practices behind the role of the digital in social research are complex and intertwined. This has led to intense debates in other disciplines as well, contributing to the development of new areas of research such as computational sociology, from digital methodology to 'big data' studies dedicated to tackling the complex array of different elements involved, such as people, technological devices, infrastructures, and data, through the elaboration of new interpretative models and empirical tools.

However, although the debate on the role of social research methods in the digital world is a new territory that opens up new perspectives of analysis, the same uses and meanings are beginning to be established and recognized in scientific discourse, starting from basic methodological concepts such as validity, reliability, and representativeness (Lombi, 2015).

An important methodological issue concerns the concept of data, which in the digital context is seen as fluid, permeable, and mobile (Lupton, 2014). The ability to extract forms of knowledge from digital data "lies in its mobility" (Leonelli, 2018, p. 13): They are in different situations and are linked to other types of information. Regarding the importance of digital data, it is also useful to use the term "trace" (Latour et al., 2012): While according to some scholars (Marres and Weltevrede, 2013; Marres, 2017) the term "data" implies a specific architecture, such as the database, the trace is more minimal and contains a reference to the specific device from which it was captured.

Another fundamental aspect is the process of digital data construction, i.e., a phase traditionally carried out by the researcher through the implementation and careful testing of data collection techniques. The construction of the empirical base has been at the centre of methodological debate over time: It is useful to recall the debates on the strengths and weaknesses of quantitative and qualitative data collection methods or, for example, on the role of biases (of the respondent or the interviewer) in the case of the structured questionnaire. In the digital context, the researcher is directly embedded in a large amount of data that seems to be already available: A typical expression of this form of empirical basis is the so-called 'user-generated content' (posts on social networks, imagines, etc.), i.e., data published by users without the presence of, for example, an interviewer. As they are not solicited from the outside, these types of data are often seen as 'natural,' promoting the idea that they provide reliable and objective forms of knowledge (Lombi, 2015). However, as Norjie Marres (2017) explains, these types of data cannot be considered natural as they are heavily formatted in terms of the technical and infrastructural characteristics of the platforms that produce and store them. Furthermore, the production of digital data is characterized by a certain opacity, as it is influenced by political, economic, social, cultural, technological, and also normative and ethical processes. In other words, the debate on methods in digital contexts is also linked to the question of the development of scientific thinking, which is understood as the result of a construction of knowledge processes that are "performed by humans and not simply discovered in the world" (Murtonen, 2015, p. 686). In the context of this discussion, Rogers (2009, p. 2) also states that digital methods seek to learn from the so-called methods of the medium, i.e., how online devices deal with web data. Digital methods are thus the study of the methods embedded in devices that handle online data.

Another point concerns a different conceptualization of the phases of empirical research, which has a less linear and sequential flow: In the quantitative method, for example, data visualisation in its function of synthesis and complexity reduction becomes a "deliberate analytical strategy rather than a technocratic method of data presentation" (Halford and Savage, 2017, p. 1139). In other words, visualisation can be seen as a means of exploring and interrogating the data as it enables the identification and communication of the configuration, patterns, and trends of variables and their relationships (Kitchin, 2014, p. 106; Halford and Savage, 2017).

While much of the discussion on digital methods focuses primarily on the techniques of data collection and analysis, there seems to be less interest in the centrality of the research questions (Neresini, 2017) and the final interpretation process (Catone and Diana, 2019b). Regarding the first point, the role of theoretical research questions is fundamental "to address an uncertainty to be reduced, i.e. to trigger the process through which data are produced and used" (Neresini, 2017, p. 14) and to try to limit the problems arising from a purely data-driven approach. Moreover, some social phenomena that can also be studied in digital contexts require the fundamental role of the social researcher, who can use their interpretative skills to make sense of a heterogeneous, unexpected multiplicity of traces and data, leading to an understanding of the relationships between seemingly unconnected information (Catone and Diana, 2019b).

All these considerations confront social scientists with the need to reconfigure traditional and new research processes and dimensions of analysis and to reaffirm the pluralism that characterizes the method of the sociological discipline (Amaturo and Aragona, 2019): This means, for example, overcoming the dichotomy of quantity or quality and identifying a complementarity between explanation and understanding that follows a layered model of knowledge and considers the matter from an integrative perspective capable of establishing continuity between inductive, deductive, and abductive reasoning (Memoli, 2004). In particular, while the debate on 'digitized methods' is gradually gaining ground as it is based on assumptions and approaches that, while different, belong to the earlier versions of traditional empirical research methods, the discussion on 'natively digital' methods requires the social researcher to adopt an interlocal stance, able to work across traditional disciplinary boundaries in order to give order and intelligibility to a variety of events that would otherwise remain too heterogeneous and therefore meaningless. From this perspective, the study of digital social research at different levels cannot be achieved by adopting a single disciplinary field but requires a broader interdisciplinary scholarly project (Neresini, 2017) that requires a profound linkage of knowledge and skills to create a common cognitive, conceptual, and linguistic framework.

In recent years, the field of digital social research has expanded significantly through contributions from adjacent disciplines, resulting in a methodological broadening that affects both analytical tools and theoretical frameworks. In particular, computational social science has emerged as a key frontier, incorporating methods from computer science, such as agent-based modelling, predictive analytics, network analysis, and machine learning, into social science inquiries. This approach allows researchers to explore complex social dynamics on a macro scale and in real time, such as the spread of opinions, misinformation, or collective behaviour on social media platforms (Lazer et al., 2009; Edelmann et al., 2020

In parallel, the adoption of artificial intelligence (AI) technologies has opened new avenues for data collection (e.g., via natural language processing or computer vision) and for interpretive analysis of large volumes of text, images, and multimedia content. However, the use of AI in social research also raises critical questions about algorithmic bias, transparency, and accountability, requiring a reconsideration of traditional categories such as validity, causality, and agency (Floridi, Cowls and Beltrametti, 2018; Mittelstadt, 2019; Ziewitz, 2016).

Another rapidly developing area is digital ethnography, which has moved beyond passive observation of online interactions to include multi-sited and multimodal methodologies. These include video-call interviews, participant observation in virtual spaces, and the collection of visual and audio materials – reshaping the very concept of "the field" (Pink, 2022; Lupton, 2020). Digital ethnographers today must navigate tensions around researcher identity, participant consent, and ethical challenges in fluid, networked spaces.

Finally, mixed methods are gaining new relevance through the possibility of combining traditional qualitative data (e.g., interviews, textual analysis) with large volumes of digital data (e.g., log files, social media metrics), often analysed using computational techniques. This convergence enables more layered and nuanced understandings of social phenomena, fostering a dialogical relationship between explanation and understanding, and between "cold" data and the meaning-making process (Creswell and Plano Clark, 2023; Gray, 2021; Molina and Garip, 2019).

Together, these emerging directions point toward an increasingly inter-disciplinary and reflexive horizon for social research – one in which technology, theory, and practice are deeply intertwined. The challenge for social scientists is not only to adopt digital tools but to actively shape and critique them, contributing to the definition of what research means in the digital age.

To summarize, the process of change and renewal that social research methods are currently undergoing entails a parallel need to update the content of teaching practice in the subject: In other words, the teaching of social research methodology should aim to educate the new generations of sociology students to a critical and conscious knowledge of the methods of empirical research, providing them with a wide range of both traditional and "new" procedures, techniques, and resources resulting from the development of digital technologies to place them in a scientific framework. Social research is in a phase of transition, and therefore, the teaching methods of this discipline should also be adapted to consider the changes that are taking place in the conceptual and empirical apparatus on which it is traditionally based.

Chapter 2

Redefining university teaching practices through ICT

2.1 The changing landscape of university education

In the last twenty years, innovations in academic teaching and the growing demand for specializations, together with the deep crisis in the intellectual labour market, have led to a wide gap being opened between the ongoing transformative forces of technology and the original foundations which were the inspiration for the tasks and aims of university education in the past. Within the current scenario, that is characterized both by a complex and variegated set of changes connected to disciplinary, pedagogical, and educational issues and to variations in the socio-cultural environment, the diffusion of Information and Communications Technology (ICT) is playing an important role in the reshaping of the educational professions in higher education (Anderson, 2005; Alvarez, Guasch and Espasa, 2009; Ammenwerth, 2017).

One of the key changes that has emerged from this development is that of the expansion and redefinition of the role of the university teacher (Calvani and Rotta, 2003; Ammenwerth, 2017) which has contributed to the rise in the number of new models of interaction between teaching, learning, and innovation: For example, teaching activities that are increasingly free from physical and temporal limits, those in which greater attention can be paid to the specific characteristics and needs of the students, as well as to changes in the social and cultural contexts of reference. Starting from these interrelated aspects, the article aims to provide a reflection on the social and cultural implications that ICT has on the teaching practices of those who work in universities.

The first section examines the overall impact that the implementation of ICT has on the work of university teachers. Among the various ICT tools and approaches, we focus on the use of e-learning as a system that can provide new teaching methods, influencing the redefinition of the work of the teachers.

The second section presents qualitative research based on unstructured interviews carried out in 2018 at the University of Salerno (Italy). The interviews were administered to 12 professors of the first-level degree course in Sociology (University of Salerno) who have been using ICT tools through e-learning platforms over the last ten years; the aim of the research was to explore their teaching experiences, in terms of their reasons for adopting an e-learning approach, the specific teaching methods they used, changes in their teaching practice and the impact of e-learning on their identity as a teacher.

The third section outlines the main results of this investigation, allowing us to identify various ways to approach and use e-learning in teaching and, more generally, how to analyse how teaching practice is being renewed to include these new developments, and how the identity of teachers is changing as a consequence of the adoption of ICT.

2.2 The role of ICT in transforming teaching practices

In recent years, the use of ICT in education has increased significantly (Harasim, 2012; Messina and De Rossi, 2015) due to the fact that it allows for the development of more open and flexible forms of teaching and learning than those found in the traditional teacher-student dynamic. Universities, despite lacking significant regulatory measures or adequate financial support (Capogna, 2014), are the most important institutions involved in this complex process (Kirkwood and Price, 2014). The use of ICT, however, involves both challenges and opportunities for the university and its teachers: the delicate relationship between tradition and innovation, i.e., between a system characterized by procedural automatisms, and one that is less structured (Colombo, 2008); the transition from a teaching model based on curricular knowledge to a more inclusive model aimed at building knowledge through the integration and negotiation of "real" and digital spaces, conceived as environments of collective and connective knowledge (Buffardi and De Kerckhove, 2011); the involvement of the students in the processes of knowledge building through ICT (Galliani, 2011); the ability to adopt more flexible learning and teaching processes that lead to a redefinition not only of temporal and spatial dimensions in which the teaching takes place, but also of all the activities involved in the work of university teachers.

Among the various methods of using ICT in higher education, e-learning, in its different approaches and modalities (full distance, blended learning, MOOC, etc.), is one of the most widely adopted systems (Garrison and Kanuka, 2004; Ranieri, 2005; Bonaiuti, 2006). In recent years, this configuration has given rise to an open debate interconnecting the pedagogical, technological, disciplinary, and social aspects (Ghislandi, Raffaghelli and Cumer, 2012) of this new way of teaching.

E-learning is considered

> an approach to teaching and learning, representing all or part of the educational model applied, that is based on the use of electronic media and devices as tools for improving access to training, communication and interaction and that facilitates the adoption of new ways of

understanding and developing learning (Sangrà, Vlachopoulos and Cabrera, 2012, p. 152).

It allows for a wide range of "presence and distance" teaching combinations, modifying the educational approach by extending the learning context beyond that of the classroom and, at the same time, changing the sequential nature of content that characterized traditional teaching methods in the past (Colombo, 2008, p. 149). The latest generation of e-learning environments is, in fact, moving towards constructivist pedagogical models (Jonassen, 1994) that place the student at the centre of the learning path through the enhancement of collaborative learning between peers (Grion, 2016) and active didactic strategies. From this perspective, e-learning systems are contributing to the changes being seen in the processes and methods of both teaching and learning, thus impacting the nature of knowledge itself and how people use and transform it (Sandrini and Colombo, 2008).

The possibility of designing and running a university course using an e-learning approach requires an overall reconstruction of the whole educational path in terms of its theoretical basis, the content to be delivered, technological choices and human resources to be employed (Trentin, 2003), in addition to an analysis of the student profile and the socio-cultural context in which the learner interacts (Diana and Catone, 2018). E-learning courses, far from being mere undifferentiated repositories of information, necessitate a careful remodelling of the design, implementation, management, and evaluation phases, through a combination of pedagogical, social, and technological components (Trentin, 2003). Within this scenario, university teachers find themselves inserted into a complex educational setting, characterized by changes related, for example, to the processes of negotiation and construction of knowledge, or the adoption of a new language. In this context, the teacher is required to know how to produce their own materials and how to regulate their work based on an integrated bricolage of activities, devices, and the varied network of people with whom they need to interact (Laurillard, 2012, p.144). When the dimension of the classroom expands on the Internet through the integration of virtual environments, space, time, and communication codes are reconfigured, affecting all the tasks and activities of the teacher (Messina and De Rossi, 2015). In other words, they are involved in a transformative process that affects the definition of their professional identity (Crotti, 2017; Arvanitis, 2018).

The process that is transforming professional identity is closely linked both to wider changes in the educational system – the increase in new forms of public management (Pompili and Viterritti, 2018) and the rise of the "entrepreneurial universities" – and to the growing demand for a more complex and interconnected set of new skills that the university teacher is required to possess. These include not only cultural, didactic, and educational skills but also specific capabilities regarding course organization, course design, and assessment, as well as social, communication, technical, and technological skills (Tammaro, Petolicchio and D'Alessio, 2017).

With regard to the latter, as mentioned above, the ongoing changes and the growing attention to the role of technologies in higher education have led to an open debate on this topic and some specific measures have been introduced at the institutional level to address the issue. Considering more specifically the field of e-learning, many public and private organizations and institutions are dealing with the subject of quality development and assurance: The European Foundation for Quality in eLearning (EFQUEL) and the European Association of Distance Teaching Universities (EADTU) are clear examples of this trend. It should also be noted here that an important role is played in this area by the standards (Learning Object Metadata, the Learning Technology Standards Committee), the recommendations of the OECD (Hénard and Roseveare, 2012), and the work of the High-Level Group on the Modernization of Higher Education. However, despite the efforts of the European Commission to promote these different types of procedures in order to "harmonize the European debate on quality in e-learning as part of a pertinent initiative" (Ehlers, 2004, p. 3), a common institutional strategy appears still to be lacking. Indeed, the results of the "E-learning in European Higher Education Institutions" survey indicate that

> despite some newly emerging initiatives, national policies and strategies for e-learning in higher education are not yet widespread and seem to enjoy only limited visibility among higher education institutions (Gaebel et al., 2014, p. 19).

According to this research, one-third of respondents stated that there is no specific e-learning policy. However, 89% of respondent institutions affirmed that they have a faculty-level strategy for e-learning. Looking at the Italian university context in particular, the survey indicates that currently there is no overall national e-learning strategy, but that there are simply some support measures at the national level.

This situation becomes even more worrying when focusing on the professional development of university teachers, given that the Italian academic system seems to lack systemic measures and strategies aimed at supporting the development of professional skills that would provide university teachers with a more critical and informed knowledge of ICT. The result is that many teachers often approach this area voluntarily, on their own initiative, or, at other times, they become directly involved in new forms of teaching following an automatic assumption that they are already qualified to use specific technological tools.

This lack of professional development is also connected to a combination of extrinsic and intrinsic factors: problems related to infrastructural and technological equipment; the organizational constraints of the university; and problems related to professional identity due to the loss of social status of the profession, age, perceptions and the attitude of teachers towards technology (Ranieri, Raffaghelli and Pezzati, 2018).

In other words, although the use of ICT and more specifically of e-learning models in higher education is developing, the training of faculty staff, regulations, as well as the organizational structure and the logistical-infrastructural conditions pose significant obstacles to a wider and more solid establishment of university teaching practices (Renzi, Klobas and Trentin, 2008). Starting from this theoretical framework, in the following sections, we report the results of qualitative empirical research aimed at investigating the use of e-learning by a group of university teachers, taking account of some of the issues outlined above.

2.3 Exploring e-learning implementation at the University of Salerno

Having briefly looked at the role that e-learning plays in higher education, below we present empirical research that was carried out in order to investigate the experiences of university professors (including former and retired professors), teaching the first-level degree course in Sociology of the Department of Political, Social and Communication Sciences (DSPSC) of the University of Salerno who had adopted e-learning systems over the last ten years. The research aims to explore the impact of e-learning on the professional development of university teachers, considering possible changes in their work, their relationships both with technology and learners, and the potential redefinition of their professional identity.

It is important to note that the DSPSC and those working on the degree course in Sociology have been involved in the design, implementation, and delivery of e-learning courses since 2001. They chose to use this approach for many reasons: to enrich the educational program, to respond to the needs of a large group of student-workers and working students, to make study paths more flexible, to try to tackle the high dropout rate, and to give students a more informed knowledge of ICT (Arcangeli and Diana, 2008). Various methods of distance learning were adopted during this extensive period, forming a development path that can be divided into three main phases.

Firstly, an experimental period from 2001-2005 in which 14 courses were delivered entirely in full distance e-learning mode, and 11 courses were offered using a blended e-learning approach – a format that integrates classroom learning time with online learning as it requires frontal lectures to be supplemented with forms of online support and activities provided by an e-learning platform (Garrison and Kanuka, 2004).

After this initial testing phase, from 2006, all the courses in Sociology were offered both in full distance mode (for students who could not attend the frontal lectures) and in a blended format.

During both of these phases, the DSPSC was supported by specialists in the fields of e-learning: an online tutor, a content designer, a multimedia developer, and a course director. Online training sessions on e-learning course design and specific training meetings were organised to allow teaching and support staff to gain more experience in the use of e-learning and to train them to become more informed in the use of the tools. All these training activities were led by a visiting professor from the California Virtual Campus. About the technological aspects, an e-learning platform called Web Course Tools (WebCT), developed by the University of British Columbia, was purchased and adopted (Yip, 2004). This platform offered the teachers a variety of tools allowing them to build their own online courses: e.g., tools for the contents (Syllabus, Dictionary, Course Content, Exercises, Simulations, Additional Readings); communication and secretarial tools (Discussion Forum, Calendar); self-assessment tasks (Self-tests) (Amendola, Errichiello and Vitale, 2005). A particularly important moment during these two phases was the winning of the "Distance Learning and E-Learning Programs - Campania 2000-2006" P.O.R. project in 2006, which was aimed at promoting the culture of distance learning and improving the quality of the didactic offer of the University of Salerno. As part of this project, funded by the Campania Region, several software programs were purchased, such as Camtasia (used for demonstrations or tutorials and to record PowerPoint presentations), Soft Chalk (to create interactive web pages), and Macromedia Studio (a suite of authoring tools).

Finally, in 2008, there was a final phase characterized by the transition from WebCT to the Moodle platform. Since then, the delivery of the course in an e-learning format has become optional and is dependent on the choice of the teacher: Ten courses were led by ten teachers and followed by an average of 70 students for each course. The decision to change the platform was taken mainly to reduce costs, since Moodle, differently from WebCT, is a free open-source platform (Nedeva, 2005). Cost considerations were followed up by an analysis of the characteristics of the platform: Moodle is recognized in the international educational context for creating user-friendly learning environments based on the sharing and co-creation of knowledge, in line with a constructivist pedagogical approach. As mentioned above, the design and implementation of the platform used by the DSPSC was entrusted to a group of e-learning experts – an online tutor, a content designer, and a multimedia developer – who shared their skills and knowledge with the course teachers. The e-learning course was therefore set up following a participative approach, taking account of pedagogical, social and technological aspects. The outcome of this process was the creation of the Des-k platform, built in the Moodle environment and characterized by various macro-areas: contents, activities, synchronous, and asynchronous communication tools (Diana and Catone, 2016).

This long three-phase development path was enriched by the highly active participation and the effort and dedication of many of the DSPSC teachers who, during this period, reflected on both the potential and the limits of e-learning by identifying more appropriate forms and contents for the educational needs of the students. Additional aspects of the project consisted of the organization of thematic seminars with colleagues from other universities, involvement in national and international conferences, participation in scientific associations in the e-learning sector, winning European projects, and investment in new human resources (designers, online tutors, etc.). In addition to this, the teachers and researchers of the DSPSC carried out many empirical analyses in order to explore the e-learning experience of those involved over these years (Amendola, Errichiello and Vitale, 2005; Arcangeli and Diana, 2008, 2009; Catone and Diana, 2016; Diana and Catone, 2016; Diana and Catone, 2018; Giordano and Vitale, 2006). While on the one hand these studies were mainly "student-centered" – i.e., focused on the analysis of the learning processes, the satisfaction level of students and the evaluation of the performance they reached – on the other hand, the point of view of the teachers in terms of their experiences and beliefs was somewhat underestimated and to a certain extent neglected.

Our qualitative empirical research was designed to fill this gap and to investigate the teaching experiences of the teachers of the degree course in Sociology who had adopted e-learning systems. The research was carried out through the use of unstructured interviews (Silverman, 2016), a technique based on the centrality of the interviewees, who thus have the opportunity to narrate and reconstruct, with the guide of the interviewer, their universe of meaning, as well as their own personal experience. From a methodological point of view, this technique, which adopts the dynamics of interpersonal communication, allows us to explore the subjective view of the interviewee in-depth and to understand their unique thoughts, beliefs, and values, at the same time encouraging a self-reflection process (Montesperelli, 1998). The interviews were carried out and recorded during the months of February and March 2018 with 12 university teachers, eight male and four females of various ages: three younger teachers (with an average age of 40 years old), five middle-aged (55 years old on average), and four elderly retired teachers (70 years old, on average). Four of them teach more applied subjects such as statistics, social research methods, social statistics, political economy; the others teach more generalist disciplines: sociology, sociology of organization, history of political thinking, contemporary history, history – remedial course and the methodology of social sciences. Due to the unstructured nature of the interview, we adopted a general line that could be adapted according to the flow of the conversation. Through the open, generative questions of the interview, we tried to address the complexity of the aim of this research, bringing to light the e-learning experience from the point of view of the teacher.

The cognitive aim of the research was operationalized in the following items that allowed us to explore and understand the e-learning experience, and in particular, the possible changes in the work of the university teacher because of the increase in the use of ICT:

⇒ The approach of the university teachers to new technologies, in terms of their reasons for using the e-learning platform, as well as their knowledge and attitudes towards e-learning.

⇒ The methods and strategies adopted in the use of e-learning: The interviewees described how they used the platform, the tools, the main resources and the process of integration between the e-learning platform and frontal lectures.

⇒ Changes in the transmission and knowledge building processes: Teachers expressed their opinion on the impact of e-learning on the students' learning process.

⇒ Aspects related to the definition of the professional identity of the teacher because of the use of e-learning, touching on the significant issue of the skills that the university teacher needs to acquire and develop and on the possible change in their status.

⇒ An overall evaluation of the experience.

After collecting the interviews, they were transcribed, analysed, and interpreted following a qualitative method (Diana and Montesperelli, 2005). In particular, the transcription was made by reporting the verbal and para-linguistic characteristics (the intonation and volume of the voice, the accents, the rhythm and speed of discourse, the pauses and their duration, etc.), through the use of conventional signals. These aspects contributed to the interpretation of the statements of the interview, which was considered a highly polysemic communicative event. Next, we developed a "reading grid": the transcripts of the interviews were grouped into classes and types, i.e., textual elements that interconnect and that assign meaning reciprocally through semantic, lexical, and grammatical relationships of proximity and contrast (Addeo and Montesperelli, 2007, p. 13).

2.4 Technological advancements and their impact on teaching methods

The analysis of the interviews revealed a complex scenario in which technological, pedagogical, social, cultural, and biographical aspects are deeply intertwined. The results we describe below should be interpreted in the light of a series of issues. First, we investigated the e-learning experience of teachers of different ages and therefore with a different level of familiarization with the technologies; moreover, the professors teach diverse subjects, and as can be seen from the results, this was a significant discriminatory factor. Finally, we considered the extensive experience of some teachers in the e-learning sector, such as the degree course in Sociology, who have been involved in the implementation of e-learning courses for over ten years; this means that the results are interpreted also taking into account the technological innovations – such as the change of the e-learning platform (from WebCT to Moodle) – that occurred during these years.

2.5 University teachers' perspectives on e-learning adoption

The first item deals with the attitude of the teachers towards e-learning, the results were varied: on the one hand, a group of interviewees (eight younger and middle-aged teachers) expressed enthusiasm, curiosity and the desire to experiment with alternative forms of teaching, exploiting the potential of ICT; on the other hand, some teachers (four older teachers) felt an initial sense of distrust towards the use of new technologies in their teaching practice.

Regarding the latter, the main reason behind the initial resistance to e-learning was due to the absence of face-to-face contact between teacher and student, as well as between students themselves. According to this group of respondents, e-learning could have hindered the social and emotional interaction on which the educational relationship has always been based, leading to significant consequences in terms of the students' level of motivation.

> I was perplexed, I didn't know what to think. In my opinion one thing that is important is that in the frontal lesson you can see their faces, you look into their eyes and understand whether they have understood or not, and you understand if they are bored. This moment of the relationship is irreplaceable, and you cannot find it in the virtual context. For this reason, I was very skeptical. (Teacher of Contemporary History - Remedial Course).

The initial approach to ICT, according to all the interviewees, followed a decision of the Department of Political, Social, and Communication Sciences to adopt e-learning in order to overcome some problems related to the irregular attendance of students, high dropout rates, cultural gaps, and difficulties related to socialization in the university context (Arcangeli and Diana, 2009). In this sense, e-learning represented an intervention strategy to support the educational path of students, keeping alive the contact with the learner and reducing these types of problems.

Among more specific reasons that led the teachers to adopt an e-learning approach, even when it was not mandatory, was the need to give more space to the practical activities that otherwise tended to be neglected for two main reasons: First, during the frontal lecture, teachers usually spend more time on explanations of theoretical aspects, precluding the opportunity to provide specific time for practical activities; second, due to the difficulty that teachers encounter in trying to follow and supervise the activities of a large number of students (Diana and Catone, 2018). This aspect emerged especially among the teachers of applied subjects (statistics, social statistics, social research methods, economic politics) who chose e-learning to have more time outside of the classroom and delegate an operative function to teaching materials and platform activities (Trentin, 2006).

A second reason for adopting e-learning was the opportunity to experiment with channels and languages that were different from the traditional ones, to establish a closer contact with the students:

> At first, I was very skeptical, but the only way to understand how e-learning worked was to actually try it out. Whilst using it, I realised that there was a very uneven, staggered level of preparation within the group of students, so there was a risk that if I did a high-level lesson, I would lose the low-level ones, and if I did a low-level lesson, those who were better prepared would get bored. In front of a large audience of students you can't go into the specifics of the problems. I wanted to understand how to find a more inclusive way of getting them to follow me. When you are in front of so many students, how can you do it? You must find different interactive formulas. (Teacher of Contemporary History).

> There is a problem of the dialogue between the teacher and the student, also for linguistic reasons given that they do not understand many of the words that we usually use. Sometimes it is not possible to establish communication with the students to get feedback, but the need for discussion and exchange is necessary in order to identify the specific needs of the student. (Teacher of Social Sciences Methodology).

Another aspect, shared by the majority (eight) of the interviewees, was the possibility to meet the needs of a significant group of students-workers and workers-students in order to give them the opportunity to choose their own times and places of study (Arcangeli and Diana, 2009).

> Using the e-learning platform, also the students who were working were integrated into a class and were part of a learning community that lasted throughout the whole degree course. (Teacher of Social Statistics).

The design of the e-learning course and, in particular, the implementation of the platform represented a delicate and challenging moment for teachers who, especially during the first years of experimentation, had been searching for new learning paths and ways to make some innovations in their teaching practices.

> The e-learning course design required a strong commitment, in the sense that ... I had to write the contents of most of the units myself; for a few units I was able to use existing material, but for almost all of the others I had to create everything from scratch. (Teacher of Political Economy).

These results show that technological innovation is an important factor of change that affects the content of courses and the skills of teachers, also since there is a more complex relationship between the level of knowledge required of new technologies and the actual knowledge of the subjects involved.

In general, during the design and implementation of the courses, the teachers were followed and supported by a group of e-learning specialists and ICT experts (an online tutor, a content designer, and a multimedia developer) who had the task of understanding the requests of the teachers – in terms of contents, objectives and activities of the courses – and implementing them in the courses.

New technologies encourage a sharing of knowledge among different professions. In this case, the specialist nature of professional knowledge becomes less important and relational skills, based on the ability to integrate different languages and skills, translating them into practical applications for problem-solving and the achievement of specific objectives, become central.

In this sense, the teaching activity is enriched with new skills and actors that enter into a relationship of communication and cooperation with the traditional teaching figures.

The negotiation between the teachers and the different professional figures involved was – as many interviewees declare – not always simple; more specifically, it was not based on the mere transposition of contents into the virtual environment, but it required a complete rethinking of the pedagogical dimension and the characteristics of the subject being taught, considering also the specific needs of the students.

> The approach to new technologies involves a reprogramming of the traditional lecture, in the sense that it is necessary to design the study

material, to establish the typology of the activities and to adapt them to the needs of the student and their skills. (Teacher of Social Statistics).

E-learning practices, in a certain sense, allowed the teachers themselves to define the teaching methods adopted, to specifically define the difficulties met by students and to identify appropriate strategies to try to overcome them.

In other words, technologies are not merely tools that the teacher develops and shapes for their own purposes, but they consist of a set of knowledge and practices, modifying the routines of structured knowledge. Within this process, the teacher activates a reflective practice linked to the ability to modify the action and to generate, in this way, a change (Giddens, 1991). In other words, technologies contribute to a "rethinking and altering one's own professional practice based on the mixing of different and complementary modes of knowing" (Arvanitis 2018, p. 117).

I had some ideas, but I didn't know how to implement them. For example, one problem was due to the lack of the "sense of the time" encountered by students. Everything that is not contemporary for them took place sometime in the past … three or three hundred years is the same thing to them. For this reason, I asked the group of designers of the platform: "How can I do this? Help me find a way to build a timeline". Starting from this need, during the design phase we developed a time machine based on the use of images. Because students these days grow up in the visual dimension. Showing them images and reconstructing a timeline is easier for them. (Teacher of History - Remedial Course).

This aspect also reflected a different level of familiarization of the teachers with the technologies according to their age, i.e., between the younger and middle-aged teachers who already have greater knowledge and expertise with the ICT, and older teachers who frequently lacked confidence and experience with these tools.

2.6 Strategies and methods in e-learning integration

The second item of the interview aims to explore the methods and strategies adopted, and different uses of the e-learning platform, depending on the learning approach chosen.

In the case of full-distance courses, the interviewees (in some cases supported by a tutor) stated that they had been actively involved in following and supervising the activities carried out by the students. The teacher was engaged in establishing and maintaining a constant dialogue with the learner to overcome the lack of communication in the frontal lecture. This led, for example, to the participation of the teacher in discussion forums, the use of synchronous teaching tools, such as the virtual classroom and the virtual conference.

Instead, in the blended courses, in which the e-learning platform is used as support for the frontal lecture, various different experiences were reported. Three teachers of statistics, social statistics, and social research methods disciplines mainly employed the platform during the frontal lecture to give information, describe situations, and use materials that would be more difficult to employ when following a more traditional teaching approach. According to them, e-learning was useful for bringing students closer to the new frontiers of social research and digital sociology (Rogers and Lewthwaite, 2019).

> During the lecture, the e-learning platform allowed me to explain the secondary data analysis, by showing students the Istat databases, the system of indicators, but also the infographics and systems to design web surveys. (Professor of Social Research Methods).

For four professors, the platform was designed to be used by students mainly at home: In the classroom, students were introduced to models, principles, and theories that they then put into practice in virtual labs, or spaces dedicated to individual and collective exercises (Bruschi and Ercole, 2005, p. 27). In this case, the teacher also played the role of facilitator and mediator between the communication flows of the classroom and the digital environment.

At the same time, two respondents acknowledged that they had moved towards a more passive e-learning approach, due to the significant workload required by the implementation of the e-learning course, using the platform mainly as a simple repository of content.

> I recognize that maybe I did not fully exploit the potential of the ICT [...] I used these e-learning tools less and less. I accept some of the responsibility for this process, in the sense that for me the overall educational commitment on all courses was already heavy, so, I preferred not to add other difficulties. (Teacher of Political Economy).

In general, the analysis of the interviews illustrates three different, interconnected ways of use of the e-learning platform. Firstly, as an opportunity to take advantage of the various languages provided by the digital environments that promote the students' learning process.

> Students could listen to music, watch film clips- things that in the classroom are more difficult to do especially now [...] there was an opportunity to mix visuals, images, art, and literature. To explain the pre-war situation, I used the anthology of Spoon River, and to explain Spoon River I used a song of Fabrizio De Andrè [...] When the students

realised that history is also Guernica and that Gramsci and Guernica are different aspects of the same political attitude, they have the possibility to open their minds, and they have fun! In the classroom, you can't easily move from the newspaper, to music, to the painting etc. Using the Internet, if you organise specific resources and materials, it is possible. (Teacher of Contemporary History).

Secondly, e-learning was adopted to foster communication: Respondents described the main tools used, such as synchronous (i.e., chats) and asynchronous (i.e., discussion forums and email) tools that promote a dialogue between peers, with the teacher and the tutor, if present.

Lastly, as mentioned above, e-learning was employed to support practical activities, through a situated design of multimedia resources, tools, and specific tasks.

The structure on which the e-learning course was built reproduces the phases that characterize the process of empirical research from the design of the research to the presentation of the results. The student, from a simulative point of view, carries out all the phases of the research involved in the study of a contemporary social phenomenon... immigration, deviance, etc. And so, they use Sociological Abstract and Google scholar for the literature review, Demo Istat platform for the collection of data [...] in practice, the student is involved in the empirical investigation, becoming aware of the activities to be carried out in order to evaluate the situations that arise over time. (Teacher of Social research methods).

According to the majority of teachers (ten in total), the e-learning course, considered as an integrated system of activities, tools, languages, and virtual and real environments, modifies the modalities of transmission and construction of knowledge: The student's learning process changes and they are placed at the centre of the knowledge production process through peer collaboration activities and the performance of authentic and contextualized tasks (Jonassen, 1994).

Chats, forums, group work, role-playing games, activities that cannot be repeated in the classroom especially if there are many students. E-learning allows students to join, to create a class, to form a mutual support network. (Teacher of Contemporary History).

At the same time, according to two middle-aged interviewees, contact with the teacher using an e-learning platform was very limited due to the lack of physical presence; in other words, the teacher is still an irreplaceable point of reference.

In the classroom you can see the faces and the expressions of the students, you can understand if they haven't understood something. If the classes are not too big, you can look at these expressions and repeat something if they haven't understood. That isn't possible in a digital environment. (Teacher of Political Economy).

Technologies, if adequately integrated, can be resources capable of bringing out new forms of critical reflexivity since they allow us to go back to the underlying rules, to internal criteria, to see problems from a plurality of perspectives and unknown angles (Calvani, 2000). The student is motivated to search for and process information of a different nature, collected from different life contexts, thus developing meta-cognitive skills, organizational skills, and social skills. (Capogna, 2014, p. 50).

Do you realise that along this path they are motivated to say, 'And then...?' and 'Why?' Students need to find bridges, to find roads, and sometimes out of prudence or laziness, we do not provide them with the directions, and the frontal lesson risks being the most convenient teaching method. (Teacher of Contemporary History).

Students understand everything they do first-hand. Because it belongs to them in a different way. What you do allows you to ask questions, it motivates your 'why'. When you just listen, the world of questions is distant. (Teacher of Social Sciences Methodology).

In this process, technological innovation is an important factor of change that affects the activities of the teachers: they moved within a more or less structured sphere of action. For some respondents, the platform determined different working hours (for, e.g., participation in discussion forums at any time of the day); for others, the e-learning platform gave greater structure and organization to their work as a teacher, as it allowed them to prepare a set of activities, resources, and materials in advance.

Doing e-learning, using ICT tools, means broadening the range of action beyond the classroom, so it means, for example, participating in discussion forums at any time of the day; it means understanding which tools allow us to attract the interest of students and which ones are useful in facilitating my work. It means reflecting and understanding. In the frontal lesson there is more improvisation. (Teacher of Social Research Methods).

During the design of the course - that was the most challenging moment for me - I had to ask myself whether my subject was suitable for the digital environment and how it could be explained through forms, contents, languages that I had never used before. In my opinion, not all subjects are suitable for e-learning. (Retired Teacher of Organizational Sociology).

The experiences described by the interviewees show how ICT tools led the teacher to undertake a reflective process, i.e., to examine their own experiences, to question their own strategies and methodologies in a context that is free from traditional physical and temporal limits and characterized by continuous changes in the social and cultural contexts of reference (Milani, Raffaghelli and Ghislandi, 2017). In other words, the adoption of ICT in teaching influences the cognitive-design structures of teachers, engaging them in the combination of disciplinary, methodological, technological, and sociocultural knowledge, as also highlighted by the research on the Technological Pedagogical Content Knowledge (TPCK) model (Mishra and Koehler, 2006; Messina and Tabone, 2014; Messina and De Rossi, 2015).

> If there is not a thinking mind behind it, there is a risk of an indiscriminate accumulation of materials. The teacher's role is central, since they organise a cultural path, a problematic path, that is not merely a multiplication of the materials. If you simply multiply them – because the Internet allows you to do this - without a specific path, it can be risky. Information does not replace the path of knowledge. We help students think, not just learn. (Teacher of History of Political Thinking).

As the following results illustrate, e-learning has not only changed the activities of the teachers, but it has also contributed to the redefinition of their role.

2.7 The influence of e-learning on teaching and learning processes

The results described above are deeply connected to certain aspects of the identity of the teacher regarding the use of e-learning. More specifically, teachers described the sensation they had of being involved in a process of change in their status. For example, the traditional asymmetry of roles, symbolized by the *ex-cathedra*, seems to have diminished. The older teachers, in fact, underlined the idiosyncrasy of technologies since they put the teacher-student dyad at risk, leading to the loss of authority in terms of

> losing control of learning processes, losing the means to monitor and control participation and interaction, or losing the role as content expert in an online learning setting (Ammenwerth, 2017, p. 3127).

This means that technological devices could influence the symbolic power of knowledge, modifying the teacher's agency to act (Holt and Segrave, 2003).

> The university teacher needs the frontal lesson because it reassures them about the power of their role. When you disappear behind a

computer, you have the feeling of having lost something. (Professor of Contemporary History).

From this perspective, the introduction of ICT in teaching could lead to a

disintegration of the educational relationships which are changing the power connection between teacher and student, within a class that appears increasingly 'liquid' since it loses the usual space and time boundaries (Capogna, 2017, p.127).

Moreover, in this context, where teaching practices are characterized by different stakeholders with different views on education and attitudes towards the use of digital devices (Salavati, 2017), new technologies could contribute to changing the institutional space (Capogna, 2016, p.64). From this perspective, in the technological world different actors

are in conflict to affirm their power and obtain legitimization: (…) national and international technology producers who try to conquer the educational technology market; governments who try to define an education policy capable of addressing the technological challenge; the supranational agencies of evaluation who emphasize the logic of benchmarking and so on. All of this reduces the margin of discretion of teachers (Capogna, 2016, p. 65).

These considerations are closely connected to the status of teachers in the ICT education setting—a subject that has generated an ongoing debate (Rienties, Brouwer and Lygo-Baker, 2013; Alvarez, Guasch and Espasa, 2009). In fact, although the use of technologies in education does not put limits on the previous roles of teachers, it does result in either a redefinition of their activities or in the addition of new roles for them (Zhu, 2011): as a course and materials designer, a knowledge constructor, a facilitator, or a coach (Ammenwerth, 2017). This model comes with expectations with regard to the social role and the work of the teacher, which seems to be experiencing a "transition from 'subject expert' to 'performance coach' in a learning situation" (Alvarez, Guasch and Espasa, 2009, p. 327).

On this point, the respondents expressed a common concern about the role of the teacher, who is still considered the depositary of specialist knowledge. Whilst on the one hand, the activities of teachers are becoming embedded in new technologies that are changing the methods and contents of their work, on the other hand, there seems to be an unwillingness to accept a radical change in their professional routines and their traditional status through the acquisition of new and different skills. According to both middle-aged and older respondents, only the acquisition of basic skills was needed in order to acquire a general knowledge of the technological innovation (Felisatti and

Serbati, 2014). Only the "basic" skills are necessary since teachers need to be supported by experts and specialists. In other words, the analysis of the interviews leads to the conclusion that the figure of the teacher, that is already subject to constant pressure due to the academic workload required of them by the managerial university, cannot be radically transformed.

> We need to develop some skills - not in the sense of technical training, but to promote awareness in order to push the teacher to consider the real effectiveness of ICT tools. (Teacher of Political Economy).

> I believe that without experienced staff, the teacher can't voluntarily ensure all the work required by e-learning is done, especially if we are talking about 120 hours of frontal teaching activities and therefore, they can't guarantee both the participation of the students in a frontal lecture and online activities. Support staff become fundamental, because otherwise our work would become very hard. (Teacher of Social Statistics).

In addition to this aspect, the new challenges for academic innovation need to be supported through training, financial resources, and acknowledgement. Indeed, the teachers believe that the use of new technologies requires a significant commitment that, at the same time, is not recognized within their careers.

> The fact that there isn't a university policy to really support these activities is a significant limitation. It is clear that if I had a member of staff specifically dedicated to e-learning, in addition to the IT experts, everything would work much better. (Teacher of the History of Political Thinking).

> In terms of costs, in terms of support, in terms of staff, because...using e-learning is an expensive activity for the structures, and it requires qualified technical staff to maintain the platforms, it requires specialized people, and the teacher cannot do all these activities. (Teacher of Organizational Sociology).

In this regard, the teachers interviewed stressed that the misalignment between institutional policies and formal recognition has a significant impact on the motivation of the teacher, who is therefore less inclined to experiment with new tools and new didactic approaches (Catelani et al., 2018, p. 769). The lack of institutional recognition also corresponds to the lack of economic benefits, since the activities carried out by the respondents were voluntary and not rewarded. These aspects can be interpreted taking into account the secondary role of teaching in the Italian university system, as the teachers are evaluated mostly based on the results of their research papers (Bruschi and Ranieri, 2018).

The combination of these criticalities has a negative effect on the effort and commitment of the teachers and on the effectiveness of the transformative process.

The issues relating to the acquisition of skills and the role of the teacher are also affected by the generational gap, since the older respondents reported encountering more difficulties in the use of new technologies, whilst the younger ones were more open and confident.

> The elderly teacher has difficulty in realigning with a system that is new to them, the young teacher is already brought up with a propensity to use new technologies and, finally we have the middle-aged teacher, who was born in an old-style generation, but is faced with a new generation of students [...] especially since now we are confronted with students who are still educated through the old system, but we will encounter students who at school have been educated using highly technological tools. (Teacher of Social Statistics).

Related to this last point, among the teachers there is an awareness of the need to stay up to date with technological innovation and to be prepared for an informed use of new tools, given that as the years go by, an increasing number of young people who enrol at university will have been trained in schools that already use digital technology, and hence universities cannot do otherwise. From this perspective, according to the majority of respondents, it is necessary to take into account the characteristics of university students (Gardner and Davis, 2014), who are inserted into a digital environment where they build their knowledge and identity. According to the majority of the teachers,

> it is necessary to intercept the semantics of their language, channeling it into a scientific framework and readjusting and transmitting in in the form of new content and knowledge, without losing the rigor and the scientific and heuristic value of knowledge (Diana and Catone, 2018, p. 158).

2.8 Redefining the professional identity of university teachers

The final part of the interview deals with the overall evaluation of the e-learning experience, in which the main strengths and weaknesses are summarized. In general, the teachers recognized many positive aspects in the use of e-learning: an increase in reflection that derives from the possibility of interfacing with constantly changing online tools; an improvement in the learning process of the student who tends to have a more active approach; and the possibility for the teacher to have greater contact with the student using participatory and collaborative methods.

However, the interviewees also identified a series of criticalities:

> There are no specific disadvantages, but there are big problems. The main problem is that, in my opinion, the university must be convinced about investing in this method of teaching. Instead, in my experience, there has always been a strong resistance to providing real support. (Teacher of Statistics).

> This experience is like a Ferrari without petrol, a greatly underused resource because it is clear that a teacher, without the support of the institution, cannot achieve significant results. (Teacher of the History of Political Thinking).

The problems encountered by respondents were therefore mainly due to the lack of institutional recognition, the difficulty – especially among older teachers – of using digital languages with ease and the increased workload that should not fall only on the shoulders of the teacher but who, instead, needs to be supported by specialized professionals. Once again, teachers stress the need to promote changes and improvements within an institutional framework that encourages their professional development through support, incentives, and recognition.

2.9 Institutional challenges and the need for support in e-learning

The research we carried out allowed us to reflect on the impact of ICT and, more specifically, of e-learning on academic teaching. In contrast to many studies that focus mainly on the learning paths of the students, this paper aims to consider this issue from the teacher's point of view. In fact, the teacher in many cases is seen solely as a transmitter of knowledge and content, almost impervious to new teaching methods and technologies. The interviews showed, on the contrary, that teachers who are involved in a path of digital innovation such as e-learning, have a great capacity and willingness to experiment with new forms of teaching; in many cases, this leads to a reshaping of the role of the teacher, who views both the contents and the relationship with learners in a different way. In other words, technological innovation represents a factor of change that influences both the actions of the teachers and their skills, thus affecting their identity as teachers.

The results of the research reveal different points: The implementation of new technologies leads to a redefinition of the specialized nature of the teacher's knowledge, through the contamination with the areas of knowledge of other professions, as well as the integration of new languages and skills; at the same time, however, according to the teachers interviewed, these changes cannot be allowed to undermine the traditional role of the teacher as the 'expert on the subject.'

The research also brought to light factors that sometimes hamper innovation, such as the fact that teachers acted predominantly on a voluntary basis, or that there is a lack of specific training on new forms of academic education, underlining the idea that it "is taken for granted" that university teaching remains "in the hands of the individual teachers" (Pompili and Viterritti, 2018, p. 34). There is a risk that exciting new opportunities for innovation will be stifled by a lack of support and recognition at the institutional level, thus undervaluing the social role of teachers.

Despite the growing attention to the theme of the quality of teaching in university education, as highlighted, for example, by the recommendations of the OECD and the work of the High-Level Group on the Modernization of Higher Education (Catelani et al., 2018), in the Italian university system, teaching takes on a secondary role compared to the results of research. As Bruschi and Ranieri (2018) state, while on the one hand, the evaluation of the quality of teaching through the definition of specific procedures is a central theme in Italian education policy, on the other hand, in the phase of national scientific qualifications (ASN), neither the commitment of teachers nor the quality of the teaching activities appear among the indicators used in the evaluation of the teaching; in other words, teaching becomes a critical element for the teacher, who is evaluated only on their performance in research activities (Bruschi and Ranieri, 2018).

We believe that in contemporary society, where digital technology poses increasingly complex and profound challenges for university education, there is a need to support professional development with integrated and innovative approaches, through policy initiatives implemented by academic institutions. To proceed in this direction, it is also necessary to consider the point of view of the subject involved in this process of transformation – in this case, the teacher – as was our aim in conducting this empirical research. This is because

> a new education policy cannot assume of technological determinism. It is not sufficient to introduce technological equipment [...] but the human and cultural factors that characterize the evolution of each techno-social environment must be carefully considered, alongside its educational implications in order to help people to use them in a correct and responsible manner in educational contexts (Capogna, 2016, p. 65).

From this perspective, it could be useful to begin a systematic collection of the reflections and assessments of teachers on their experiences and practices using ICT in the public university system. One interesting example of this is the EduOpen portal (www.eduopen.org), which hosts e-learning courses held by Italian teachers from many subject areas and representing excellence in scientific research. The sharing of these platforms would certainly give the academic teaching staff greater support by providing a community with which to compare methods and experiences.

Chapter 3
Teaching digital research methods

3.1 The necessity of a multidimensional approach

Addressing the core issues and discussions around teaching social research methods, the challenges faced by students, and the emerging trends in social research, this chapter shares our teaching experiences during the 2018/19 and 2019/20 academic years. I focus on the development and implementation of two university courses at the University of Salerno, Italy. These educational initiatives stem from a decade-long process of reflecting, designing, implementing, and evaluating e-learning courses in the methodological field (Arcangeli and Diana, 2009; Diana and Catone, 2016; 2018; Catone and Diana, 2017; 2019a; 2019c).

The first course, "Social Research Methodology," is a 60-hour course offered in the second year of the bachelor's degree in Sociology, awarding nine credits. During the second semester of the 2018/2019 academic year, approximately 110 students enrolled.

This course aims to equip students with the knowledge, skills, and vocabulary necessary to design quantitative social research projects. Specifically, it teaches students to translate a general social problem into a specific research question, transform abstract concepts into measurable ones, and develop an understanding of data collection and analysis techniques in social research. The goal is to foster methodological expertise in quantitative research, enabling students to conduct research (define appropriate research designs, lead data collection and analysis, and link results to initial hypotheses) and critically evaluate others' research studies (Meraviglia, 2004).

The second course, "Open Data for Social Research," was offered in the first semester of the 2019/2020 academic year to 16 students pursuing a master's degree in Sociology and Policies for the Territory. Unlike the first course, this advanced course focuses on equipping students with the knowledge and tools needed to manage new types of data that can be freely used, reused, and redistributed according to licensing guidelines. The rise of the Internet and new technologies has enhanced transparency in public administrations, making previously administrative data public and reusable, thus promoting civic engagement and democratic participation based on transparency (Diana and Ferrari, 2023, 2024). This course introduces students to digital methods as new frontiers in social research, enabling them to understand the construction and analysis of digital information. Students also engage in digital research projects, integrating digitally acquired information with traditional data collection methods.

Designing a university course is a multifaceted process that considers pedagogical, social, technological, and subject-related aspects (Diana and Catone, 2018). Shulman's Pedagogical Content Knowledge model highlights the importance of a teacher's knowledge in course design, encompassing subject content and pedagogical strategies (Shulman, 1987). Teachers should present course content innovatively, using various activities, emotions, metaphors, and exercises to enhance student understanding. Further developments, such as the Technological Pedagogical Content Knowledge model (Koehler and Mishra, 2005, 2008), include understanding student profiles, socio-economic-cultural contexts, and integrating technology into pedagogy. In designing these courses, I considered all these dimensions to create an educational path tailored to the specific, contextualized needs of learners.

I adopted a constructivist approach, emphasizing active and constructive student roles in their learning processes. This educational model views knowledge as a dynamic product of personal experiences and interactions with teachers and peers (Farkas, 2012). It aligns with contemporary societal transformations that require active learning skills and adaptability (Beck, 1992; Bauman, 2006). Constructivist learning environments reflect real-world complexities, providing multiple representations of reality and encouraging reflective and context-dependent knowledge construction (Jonassen, 1994). Our course design aimed to place students at the centre of the knowledge-building process through real-world cases, fostering critical reflection and meta-cognitive processes.

Understanding the socio-economic and cultural context in which students operate, and their knowledge and skills levels, is crucial for designing quality learning processes. Our courses catered to students in Campania, a region in southern Italy with significant historical, demographic, economic, and social challenges. High poverty rates, unemployment, and lower educational attainment levels compared to national averages affect students' university experiences. These contextual factors influenced our course objectives, as they impact students' educational trajectories.

Undergraduate social research methodology courses often attract students with inadequate study methods and literacy and numeracy challenges (Gal et al., 2009). Conversely, Master's students are typically more prepared, autonomous, and flexible, often balancing work and studies. This generation of students is highly socialized with digital devices, shaping their identity, communication, and knowledge acquisition through the web (Palfrey and Gasser, 2008; Auster, 2016). Our course designs incorporated strategies to accommodate these diverse needs and skill levels, ensuring flexible learning trajectories that balance methodological rigor with students' specificities.

Another key dimension of a multidimensional approach to teaching digital social research involves equipping students with technical and infrastructural competencies that align with contemporary data practices. As digital social research increasingly requires the handling, analysis, and visualisation of complex data, familiarity with tools such as Python and R for data manipulation and statistical modelling (Wickham and Grolemund, 2016), and Gephi for social network analysis and graph visualisation (Bastian, Heymann and Jacomy, 2009), becomes essential. These platforms are not only widely used in academic research but also highly adaptable for teaching purposes, enabling students to engage with real-world datasets and develop practical, transferable skills (Van Atteveldt and Peng, 2018).

Introducing these tools into coursework requires appropriate technological infrastructure, including access to computational environments, open-source software, cloud-based platforms such as JupyterHub and RStudio Server, and collaborative repositories like GitHub. Effective data practices also depend on teaching students how to organise and manage data systematically, even when using basic tools such as spreadsheets (Broman and Woo, 2018). Moreover, embedding these tools into applied research projects fosters a hands-on learning model, where students can experiment, iterate, and reflect on methodological decisions. This integration ensures that students are not only conceptually aware of methodological innovation but also capable of navigating the technical and procedural dimensions of contemporary social research.

3.2 Implementing digital learning in higher education

Considering the intricate combination of pedagogical, disciplinary, and social aspects identified earlier, I have deeply reflected on how to implement and deliver the Social Research Methodology and Open Data for Social Research courses to align with the educational objectives, effectively support student learning, and create an educational path suited to their needs. During the design phase, I evaluated different strategies, including blended learning, which uses an e-learning platform to support in-person lessons. This method seemed most appropriate given the subject matter, the constructivist approach adopted, and the specific characteristics of the students' profiles. This decision was also informed by previous e-learning experiences in the sociology degree course at the University of Salerno, which has designed and implemented both blended learning and fully online courses for over ten years. The Social Research Methodology course, through continuous experimentation, has been delivered in various e-learning formats for some time (Arcangeli and Diana, 2009; Diana and Catone, 2016; 2018; Catone and Diana, 2017; 2019a; 2019c). The Open Data for Social Research course was delivered for the first time in the 2019/20 academic year using a blended model that included constructing and using an online platform to support in-person lessons.

Over the past few decades, the impact of the Internet and Information and Communications Technology (ICT) on education (Dabbagh and Bannan-Ritland, 2005; Ehlers, 2013) and the shift from communication as 'information' to 'participation' (Capogna, 2014) have significantly contributed to the development of e-learning. E-learning, generally defined as using various online technologies to facilitate and support knowledge acquisition, has evolved from simply conveying traditional content more efficiently to encompassing a broader conception that includes technical skills, cognitive, and relational components (Capogna, 2014). Designing and implementing an e-learning environment is complex and involves theoretical and technological choices and decisions regarding human resources (Beetham and Sharpe, 2007; Ehlers and Pawlowski, 2006; Kirkwood and Price, 2014; Lupton, Mewburn and Thomson, 2017).

The debate on using e-learning and ICT in higher education is extensive (Rosenberg, 2001; Colombo, 2008; Njenga and Fourie, 2010; Rennie and Morrison, 2013). This debate has intensified recently as social, historical, and cultural conditions increasingly require adopting new systems for creating knowledge and skills that transcend the traditional constraints of place and sequential content typical of 'in-person' education. The COVID-19 pandemic has underscored the need for e-learning systems to ensure educational continuity across all levels, from primary schools to universities (Diana, Ferrari and Dommarco, 2021; Radha et al., 2020; Rapanta et al., 2020).

E-learning's multidimensional nature affects different perspectives of analysis, emphasizing the role of technology in higher education (Webb and Cox, 2004; Kirkwood and Price, 2014), its effects (Tamim et al., 2011), and its weaknesses (Bingimlas,2009). Despite the increasing number of studies on e-learning, empirical research supporting the benefits of digital technologies is limited and lacks common methodologies, definitions, classifications, and guidelines for evaluating ICT's role in education (Pandolfini, 2016). Considering the educational system's complexity, a systematic and broader approach is needed to explore various dimensions of analysis, including a macro level concerning national and local policies and access to infrastructure and digital resources, a meso-level focusing on institutional environments, and a micro level dealing with teacher and student practices and outcomes (Pandolfini, 2016).

In recent years, there has been significant development in designing and implementing ICT and e-learning systems in higher education to achieve various goals, such as providing more flexible teaching and learning approaches, addressing low attendance and high dropout rates, expanding participation in higher education, and preparing students for technologically and digitally advanced environments (Kirkwood, 2009, p. 107).

The contemporary e-learning scenario is moving towards a constructivist approach that emphasizes acquiring knowledge over mere transmission. This approach is centred on the student, customized content, and collaborative environments involving co-production processes (Harasim, 2012). The main objectives of e-learning include stimulating critical thinking; encouraging the emergence of tacit knowledge in terms of procedures, social interactions, and cultural values; fostering learning by doing through practical application of theoretical knowledge; finding and organizing information from various sources; and promoting active participation, dialogue, and collaboration among students (Arcangeli and Diana, 2009). E-learning environments are designed to create new situations and contexts that improve scientific thinking and foster motivation (Corazza, 2006) by encouraging practical activities, role-playing, collaboration (Dabbagh, 2005), and reflective processes where students reconstruct their views and interpret their world through frequent conversations (Laurillard, 1995). These online environments provide multiple means of representation, expression, and engagement to accommodate different learning styles and increase motivation.

However, e-learning also has limitations, such as requiring more attention and concentration from students, sometimes being perceived as boring, limited communication between instructors and students, and challenges in ensuring students complete courses. These constraints can lead to lower teaching and learning efficiency. Additionally, developing e-learning platforms involves critical issues related to the datafication of teaching in higher education, affecting learning and teaching processes (Williamson, Bayne and Shay, 2020).

As traditional classroom learning and pure e-learning each have strengths and weaknesses, the latest trends are moving towards a blended model that combines the strengths of face-to-face learning with online formats. Blended learning integrates synchronous and asynchronous formats (Geer, 2009) and can take various forms, such as reducing class activities and replacing them with online activities or supplementing in-class activities with digital technologies (Auster, 2016, p. 40). Blended learning's added value lies in maintaining the traditional values of face-to-face teaching while integrating online learning advantages, thus enhancing the learning process through diverse communication forms.

This educational approach views learning as a continuous process, allowing students to become autonomous learners outside the classroom (Ma'arop and Embi, 2016). In adopting a blended learning approach, I considered its advantages, such as supporting frontal lectures with laboratory paths to encourage project-based learning (Ranieri, 2005). These platforms generally provide easier access to study materials, more opportunities for dialogue, active participation in communities, collaborative learning, and the ability to complete activities and projects based on authentic practice, drawing on the strengths of the learning community (Taylor, 2002). However, blended learning also has limitations, such as students' computer illiteracy, lack of access to personal computers (Al Zumor et al., 2013), and the need for motivation and effort to engage in both in-person and online activities.

3.3 Integrating digital learning with traditional teaching

Having examined the role of technology in education and the main features of e-learning and blended learning systems, I will now describe the structure of the Social Research Methodology and Open Data for Social Research courses, with a particular focus on the designed and implemented online platforms. These courses involved various stakeholders: the teacher, who conducted the lectures and managed the online activities; the students; and the tutor, who supported students in using the platform. The courses have distinct cognitive objectives – Social Research Methodology is an introductory course on social research methodology and techniques, while Open Data for Social Research is an advanced and specialized course. Therefore, the content, resources, tools, and online platforms were developed differently to account for these specificities.

3.3.1 Experience in a basic social research methods course

The Social Research Methodology course is structured simply and linearly to provide students with a clear and rigorous introduction to basic methodological concepts. Initially, the course content is demonstrated and explained in the classroom by the professor. Subsequently, students can study the subject in more depth and integrate their learning through the e-learning platform. This platform enhances the face-to-face course and complements traditional textbooks, which remain essential educational tools guiding and structuring the learning process.

The e-learning platform was built using Moodle, a free and open-source course management system popular among higher education professors. It offers a flexible, modular, and user-friendly learning space that allows teachers to create, organise, and provide course materials, resources, and collaborative activities following a socio-constructivist approach (Gogan, Sirbu and Draghici, 2015). The course contents are organised into units, released on the platform according to the topics discussed during the lectures, simulating the typical path of social empirical research. This path follows a sequence of procedures and actions that researchers undertake to achieve their research aims: starting from theory, progressing through data collection and analysis phases, and returning to theory with the presentation of results.

The design phase focused on identifying the logical and conceptual framework underpinning empirical research and translating this into an e-learning environment (Diana and Catone, 2018). By engaging in the activities provided for each phase, students simulate and conduct empirical research on contemporary social phenomena. The e-learning platform offers students hands-on experience with real-life tasks, enabling them to "live" the entire research process, from defining a theoretical problem to interpreting results. This structure allows students to gain a comprehensive understanding of the subject.

Additionally, the e-learning platform introduces students to new web resources, tools, and techniques for social research, providing easier and more direct access to these resources and guiding them toward a more informed and aware use of knowledge. The platform represents a direct channel that guides and supports learners in understanding and using the digital resources needed for social research.

The stages of the empirical process offer an ideal path that students can follow with flexibility, often characterizing empirical investigations.

Each unit contains three interrelated sections:

Course content and topics: Developed using interactive and digital resources, this section bridges and connects with the theoretical content explained by the professor in the classroom.

Activities: This includes exercises, simulations, case studies, and micro-projects that allow students to practice the content acquired in the classroom and explore it further on the online platform.

Tools, resources, and materials: This provides the necessary tools, resources, and materials needed to carry out activities for each phase of empirical research.

The combination of these sections creates a coherent learning process, encouraging learners to integrate and connect cognitive questions, research strategies, and techniques critically. Additionally, thematic sections make the platform dynamic and flexible, familiarizing students with social research as an open and creative cognitive process rather than an automatic validation of pre-formulated ideas (Bailyn, 1977). Students can follow the provided steps or explore different paths through specific in-depth areas provided by the e-learning environment, helping them achieve cognitive goals.

This platform structure centres students in the knowledge production process, encouraging them to create, discover, apply, and innovate, seeking both conceptual and practical knowledge for quantitative research. Moreover, the platform provides examples of contemporary social phenomena (e.g., migration, employment) and case studies relevant to sociology students, emphasizing the value of quantitative research for both sociological practice and active citizenship (Payne and Williams, 2011).

The first unit focuses on research design, where cognitive objectives are defined, and concepts are empirically translated. This step includes all design activities preceding field access, identifying procedures to address the chosen problem. The platform supports students in choosing a research theme, defining study aims, properties, units of analysis, space-time context, methodological orientations, and research strategies. They are guided in developing a literature review, retrieving sociological theories, identifying statistical sources, and reconstructing the phenomenon's evolution. Specific external resources are recommended, such as Scopus, Google Scholar, Sociological Abstracts, and Social Sciences Citation Index (Corbetta, 2003).

Using these resources, learners develop conceptual maps, selecting general dimensions and related concepts. They use acquired theories and knowledge to identify hypotheses connecting different concepts. Concept maps establish semantic associations between concepts, visually organise them, and stimulate cognitive and meta-cognitive skills necessary for managing complex phenomena (Vidotto Fonda, 2016). Digital maps created using tools like Mindomo, CmapTools, Mindmeister, and Inspiration offer additional functionalities such as editing, revision, sharing, and collaborative construction.

Next, students choose methodological procedures and specific data collection techniques. Gamification activities simulate typical constraints during empirical research, helping students understand their impact on the research process and manage unforeseen events (Urh et al., 2015). These activities develop students' methodological knowledge, choice of techniques, and ability to adapt existing methods (Marradi, 2007).

After defining cognitive objectives and research strategies, students construct the empirical basis by collecting information using appropriate techniques. The platform guides primary data collection through web surveys and secondary data collection through links to national and international databases. It introduces interactive digital resources like the OECD's "The Better Life Index," allowing students to visualize and compare key factors contributing to well-being.

After constructing the empirical basis, students organise the collected data into matrix structures. The platform provides tutorials for data entry and coding, integrating different databases. Data analysis activities follow, using tools like PSPP and Excel. Students choose analysis techniques suited to their cognitive objectives and perform data analysis exercises. Finally, students present data using tools like PowerPoint and Tableau.

These activities are supported by self-assessment tests, shared documents, interactive exercises, and quizzes, promoting collaborative learning among peers. Forums activate collaborative learning, with some managed by teachers or tutors and others by students, such as the "online café." The multimedia section includes a "cinema and social research" area with YouTube links to film excerpts illustrating social research tools, fostering methodological reflection and understanding of scientific methods (Gobo, 2009).

3.3.2 Experience with an advanced course in social research methods

The second course, Open Data for Social Research, was conducted through a combination of in-person lectures and Google Classroom, a free web-based learning management platform that enables professors to create and manage classes using user-friendly tools and collaborative activities (Harjanto and Sumarni, 2019). This service, part of the Google Suite for Education, has been offered by the University of Salerno since 2019 through an institutional partnership with Google. Unlike the Moodle platform used in the Social Research Methodology course, which students primarily accessed from home for in-depth study and practice, the Google Classroom platform is an integral part of the in-person lessons. The course takes place in a computer lab, allowing students to develop content and use the platform's resources and tools during the lecture.

Google Classroom allows teachers to create content (pictures, videos, links), organise activities, and manage administrative duties. It is structured into three main sections: stream, classwork, and people. The stream section is a collaborative space featuring a dynamic forum where students and teachers can interact by posting announcements and messages. The classwork section is the main page where teachers organise the course into modules and thematic units enriched with content, activities, and learning tools. The people section contains information about all the students and teachers enrolled in the class.

The course themes are organised into two main modules under the classwork section: The first module introduces digital methods, providing the broader context for open data, while the second module delves into the specific topic of open data. Both modules consist of integrated combinations of digital and interactive content enriched with audio, video, and graphics, collaborative activities, and tools provided through external links.

The first module begins with examples and practical cases highlighting the datafication processes of digital society. Students are guided through understanding the main challenges of conducting research in digital environments. All resources and activities are designed to give them experience in the various cyclical and interrelated phases of digital social research, which follow each other in a less linear and more networked manner, repeating and overlapping.

The initial step involves formulating a research project that considers the availability of digital traces, data, and information from the web. Unlike primary data collected directly by researchers, social research in digital environments typically involves secondary information available online. Students need to learn how to formulate appropriate research questions by connecting different types of empirical bases.

Caliandro and Gandini (2019) note that in digital research, formulating the research question is linked to awareness of constraints posed by data and digital contexts. Students must understand the non-neutrality of digital environments, as digital data are often not produced in a scientific research context but are structured for other purposes.

To understand the characteristics of empirical bases in digital contexts and connect the available information with research questions, students explore and observe online platforms (databanks, social networks, etc.) from a qualitative perspective. This allows them to critically understand the various aspects underlying the construction of information and the types of information identified (numerical, textual, visual, etc.). The task is to make students aware of the problems and methodological issues of data construction in digital environments, which are often highly formatted according to the technical and infrastructural characteristics of the platforms that generate and store them (Marres, 2017).

Students learn to use basic scraping techniques with commands from R data analysis software and more user-friendly interfaces and apps for interactive content extraction. Tools such as the Twitter Capture and Analysis Toolset (DMI-TCAT) and Netvizz (Rieder, 2013) help capture digital traces and metadata. They are guided in exporting data into structures like matrices and performing specific data analyses using data analysis software. These phases include continuous information interpretation activities.

3.3.3 Deep dive into open data

The second module focuses specifically on open data. Students are introduced to open data through exploration of major online platforms at both national and international levels. They then engage in a research project on a contemporary social phenomenon chosen by the students themselves. This practical research experience fosters the development of civic and social skills, promoting active citizenship, democratic participation, legality, territorial identity, collaboration, initiative, curiosity, critical analysis, and digital skills related to the conscious use of new technologies.

The chosen research topic is developed through the formulation of research questions, data collection, analysis, and presentation of results. A central task involves the exploration and use of open data datasets. Through a hands-on approach, students identify different types of open data and analyse the methodological characteristics of this information. They extract and combine datasets; analyse statistical indicators, indices, and ratios; and apply specific multidimensional analysis techniques. Students learn to use visualisation tools like Tableau and Infogram to present data interactively on the web. Effective data analysis and visualisation are critical in contemporary social research, where accessible data and tools enable high-quality analytical and graphical work (Healy and Moody, 2014). The ability to link data and digital traces and provide interactive, intuitive visualisations often coincides with the analysis process, as visualisation aids in synthesizing and simplifying complex data.

The final product of this module is a comprehensive report encompassing all stages of the research process. To support students in these activities and develop their methodological competence regarding open data, the platform includes a specific section with work materials and various external open data resources, giving students direct access to databases. Emphasis is placed on the information collection phase, where key open data platforms are identified and described. These platforms include the open databanks of the Italian public administration, the Italian Ministry of Cultural Heritage and Activities and Tourism (MiBACT), Open Coesione, Dati Open, and international platforms like the EU Open Data Portal, European Data Portal, Open Data Monitor, European Open Data, and the Open Data Barometer by the World Wide Web Foundation.

The materials section also provides video tutorials and guides on using software like Excel, SPSS, and Tableau to assist learners in data collection and analysis procedures. Additionally, free digital resources such as the Open Data Handbook, which addresses the legal, social, and technical aspects of open data, are available.

A key feature of both modules is the collaborative approach, encouraged through synchronous and asynchronous tools that facilitate communication between peers, teachers, and tutors, activating knowledge generation processes. Discussion forums allow students to experiment with accumulated knowledge and test the adequacy of their methodological language. Students work in groups of three or four to complete activities using shared Google documents, enabling collective participation and interaction on the same pages. This collaborative work allows students to share experiences, negotiate understanding, and build mutual knowledge, assisting each other in the online learning process. Each group participates in peer assessment, evaluating other groups' projects and providing feedback. This metacognitive process promotes methodological expertise, critical thinking, and self-awareness (Chao, Saj and Hamilton, 2010).

Another collaborative activity involves creating a methodological glossary, where students collect, organise, and define new concepts related to digital empirical research. Unlike the predominantly oral communication in frontal lectures, these online activities emphasize writing, considered a powerful articulation and representation of thought (Harasim, 2012). Writing encourages reflection and awareness, fostering a deeper understanding of course topics. The use of multiple communication modes – oral during lectures and written, visual, and interactive through digital environments – aligns with the preferences of new generations of students, enhancing their comprehension of the course material.

Chapter 4
Digital learning and visualisation

4.1 Research design and methodology

After discussing the design and implementation of the Social Research Methodology and Open Data for Social Research courses using a blended learning model, this chapter presents the main findings of two empirical studies: The first aims to understand students' e-learning experiences (para. 3.1, 3.2), and the second focuses on the impact of teaching and learning data visualisation in social research methodology courses (para. 3.3, 3.4).

Although these insights cannot capture all the complexities of the learning journey, examining the courses from the students' perspective provides valuable information about opportunities and strengths, and how they perceive the educational process as beneficial for their professional growth (Marzano, 2012). According to the 'Students' Voice' approach (Ghislandi and Raffaghelli, 2013), it is crucial for students to actively participate in constructing their learning spaces through open, co-constructed, collaborative, and reflective processes between teachers and students (Ghislandi and Raffaghelli, 2013, 273).

For the university courses discussed, the learner experience was investigated through two different research studies that considered the specificities of both courses in terms of subject matter, learning objectives, student profiles and capabilities, and the characteristics of the e-learning platform used.

The following section presents the main results of the empirical investigation related to the Social Research Methodology course, conducted using a quantitative method. Specifically, a standardized questionnaire comprising 18 closed-ended questions was administered anonymously via Google Forms to 88 students attending the course. The questionnaire was designed to investigate various aspects of the blended course experience, such as students' knowledge and attitudes towards e-learning; their study methods using the platform, tools, and resources; and the impact of the e-learning platform and tools on their acquisition of methodological expertise.

For the Open Data for Social Research blended course, to gain deeper insights into students' opinions and evaluations, a qualitative approach was chosen, based on creating two focus groups. A total of 16 respondents were divided equally into two groups of eight, with two male and six female students in each group. The main results are illustrated in the first part of this chapter (para. 4.1, 4.2).

Compared to other qualitative techniques, focus groups seemed the most appropriate choice, as their generative questions favoured knowledge sharing, perspective sharing, and self-reflection among students who had a common learning experience. The cognitive aims of the research were operationalized into items that allowed exploration and understanding of the e-learning experience: the use of technologies in university study; evaluation of the e-learning experience with respect to tools, activities, relationships with teachers and peers; acquisition of methodological expertise related to open data; and social research in the digital context. Each focus group was led by the teacher with the support of an observer to facilitate question formulation, discussion, and data collection. After the focus group sessions were completed, the dialogue contents were transcribed, noting both verbal and para-linguistic characteristics, and subsequently organised into categories and classes selected through semantic associations of proximity and contrast. Finally, these transcripts were analysed and interpreted using a hermeneutic approach based on a qualitative method (Diana and Montesperelli, 2005; Addeo and Montesperelli, 2007).

4.1.1 Activities and tools in acquiring methodological skills

The respondent group was predominantly female (82.2%) compared to male (17.8%), reflecting the composition of students enrolled in the Sociology degree at the University of Salerno. Most of them spend an average of two to four hours on campus outside lesson times (*Figure 4.1*).

Figure 4.1. Thinking about your typical week, outside of class hours, how many hours do you spend on average on Campus?

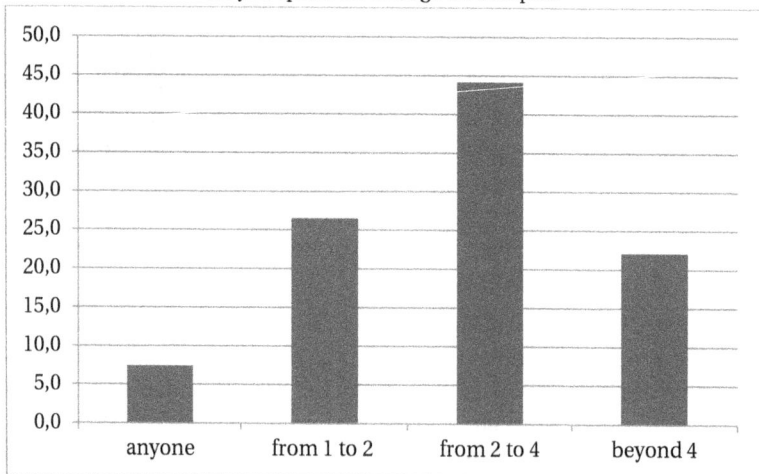

Another significant aspect found in other surveys was the employment status of students, with 36.5% identifying as working students. This circumstance not only influences how the data is interpreted but also highlights the need for a more flexible learning path that is not confined to traditional space-time dimensions, given the likelihood of irregular attendance by these students. *Figure 4.2* shows that the majority of students opted for the Bachelor's degree program in Sociology during their final year at school, but a significant number of students only made this decision a few weeks before the enrolment deadline.

Figure 4.2. When did you decide to enroll in the degree course in Sociology?

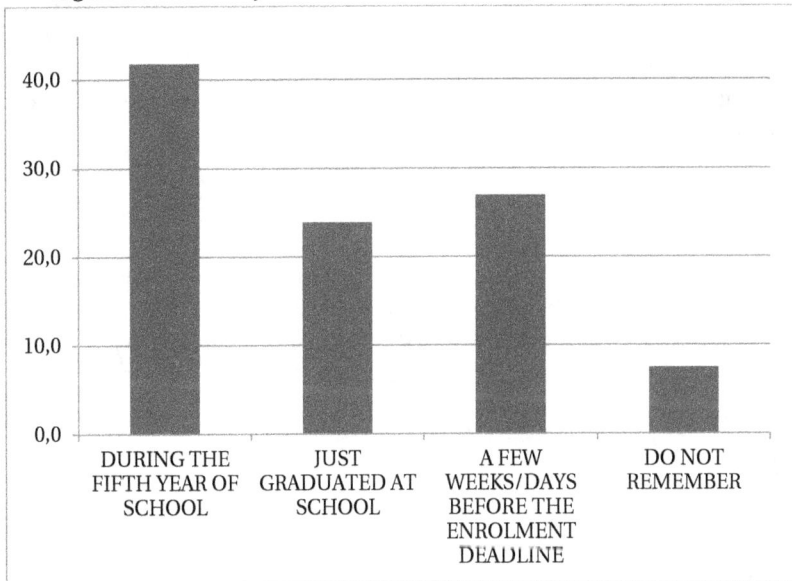

In an introductory section of the questionnaire, students were asked to assess the importance of the Internet in their everyday life and their study activities. On a scale from 0 to 10, the Internet received an average score of 8.4, although this figure decreased to 7.2 when contextualized in study activities. Despite the gap between daily life and study use, this result underscores the importance of the Internet in study activities, indicating forms of self-regulated learning.

A central issue of this investigation was the evaluation of platform-supported activities through digital technologies. I was particularly interested in assessing tasks included in each e-learning platform unit related to the simulation of empirical research, encompassing all phases from formulating the research question to presenting the results. Our questions focused on whether the e-learning platform supported the learning process concerning the multiplicity of issues, procedures, rules, and practices underlying social research.

The responses indicated that conducting research simulations using the platform's digital resources and activities was very useful for several reasons: practicing theoretical concepts addressed in the classroom (84.2% said enough or a lot), understanding contemporary societal issues through scientific reasoning rather than common sense (63.4% said enough or a lot), fostering curiosity about social phenomena (71.2% said enough or a lot), and approaching the use of digital resources in social research (66.7% said enough or a lot). These results show that making research visible and allowing students to create the entire investigation process using digital resources centres them in the learning process rather than being passive observers. However, the lower value related to understanding the complex relationship between scientific reasoning and common sense in a basic Social Research Methodology course highlights an important cognitive challenge for students, emphasizing the method's value and role, which oscillates between rules and choices.

The Social Research Methodology course, focusing on the quantitative method, was designed with the idea that digital technologies in an e-learning environment could enhance methodological skills related to numeracy and quantitative reasoning in analysing social phenomena. This subject matter, as discussed in the first chapter, presents critical learning points. Through a *Cantril scale*[1] from 0 to 10, students evaluated how much platform activities helped them acquire various components underpinning methodological competence.

The average scores indicated that platform activities and resources were particularly valuable for acquiring skills such as analysing quantitative data (7.2), reading and interpreting tables (7.8), and presenting and visualising data (7.7), understood as correct graphic representation according to variable nature and complexity reduction. Comfortingly, the high score for quantitative data analysis suggests that practical platform activities helped reduce students' typical prejudices about statistical concepts and fostered confidence and awareness through less rigid learning times and spaces. The lowest score (6.3) was for identifying, selecting, and organizing secondary data, reflecting difficulties in managing information overload and navigating secondary data mines with methodological rigor. These results align with final evaluations indicating students' greatest challenges in constructing the empirical research basis through accurate, reflective attitudes towards information (Messina and

---

[1] The *Cantril Scale*, also known as the *Cantril Self-Anchoring Scale*, is an instrument used in survey research to measure people's perceptions of their current and future well-being. Respondents are asked to visualise a ladder with steps numbered from 0 to 10, with the top step representing the best possible life and the bottom step representing the worst possible life. They are then asked to rate their current life and their expectations for the future on this scale.

De Rossi, 2015). Evidently, greater teacher support was needed during these cognitive processes.

The issue of competencies is crucial, as digital technologies in an e-learning environment can foster numeracy and quantitative reasoning by developing digital skills (Catone and Diana, 2019a). Digital competence involves exploiting information society technologies for work, leisure, and communication with a critical mindset, supported by basic ICT skills such as using computers to find, evaluate, store, produce, present, exchange information, and participate in collaborative networks via the Internet (European Parliament and the Council, 2006). Digital competence can be integrated into quantitative research phases in digital contexts through acquiring literacy skills requiring technological, critical, cognitive abilities, and an ethically responsible Internet attitude (Menichetti, 2017): ICT literacy, information literacy, Internet literacy, media literacy, visual literacy, and digital literacy (Ala-Mutka, 2011). These literacies contribute to empirical investigation in increasingly digitized social research scenarios, where information is closely linked to the platform generating and storing it, creating a virtuous interconnection between digital and numeracy skills (Catone and Diana, 2019a).

Another survey section explored the tools and materials students used most frequently. Students rated materials on a scale from 0 (min. use) to 10 (max. use). The most frequently used materials were datasets, questionnaires, worksheets, guidelines (7.6); external links (7.2); and quizzes and multiple-choice exercises (8.6). Students often requested more practice exercises, particularly in quantitative data analysis, to self-evaluate and prove skill acquisition. Videos (5.6) and discussion forums (4.5) received lower values, indicating that despite the platform's collaborative activity design, students generally used it individually. This aligns with findings that 45.4% of respondents did not view the platform as a socializing environment, suggesting a need for discussion on peer collaboration in different learning environments.

The variety of resources on the e-learning platform enables students to engage in hands-on tasks, examine activities from multiple perspectives, and seek knowledge and solutions through an 'inquiry method.' The tools and materials act as a 'toolkit' for research processes, promoting situated and contextualized learning for a better understanding of empirical research design in sociology. Students rated exercises highly (7.4) for reflecting on and understanding difficulties, as they could review and analyse their performance. Multimedia and external links helped understand subjects and expand on classroom information (6.2).

Evaluating the platform's graphic and visual dimensions is crucial in digitally mediated learning. Visual communication, supported by clear didactic design, maintains student attention, fosters curiosity, and helps absorb fundamental concepts. Students rated the visual and graphic unit structure as stimulating (6.8) and user-friendly (7.2), with images (graphs, diagrams, charts, concept maps) being particularly useful (6.9). Visual tools foster information analysis and processing skills, drawing inferences, and providing abstraction (Bobek and Tversky, 2016), while encouraging motivation and attention (Reilly, Ring and Duke, 2005).

Survey results highlight how the platform supports and transforms study methods, emphasizing e-learning's active role in redefining learning processes and modes (Colombo, 2008). About 65.4% of students found it useful for adopting a more flexible study approach regarding time and place, benefiting from readily accessible materials. Importantly, a final questionnaire question underscored the value of e-learning combined with face-to-face lessons. Most respondents found the blended course effective, with both in-class and online activities, while a purely distance format would have been difficult and less interesting (69.8%). Students (74.3%) also emphasized the teacher's role as a facilitator and mediator between classroom and digital environment communication flows, supporting practical e-learning activities introduced through theoretical classroom concepts. This result underscores the teacher's central role in content delivery and organizing learning times, adapting to students' progress across teaching units.

4.1.2 Exploring students' use of technology for study

To gain a comprehensive understanding of students' learning paths in the Open Data for Social Research course, I first examined their general use of technology for study activities. This investigation was followed by an analysis of the specific experiences students had during the course, focusing on the interplay between the disciplinary and conceptual aspects of the subject and the technological and pedagogical components, as perceived by the students.

Analysing the results from our study on the general use of technology in learning, the two focus groups revealed different, interconnected ways in which technology is used for studying. Some students indicated that their use of digital resources is typically linked to the subject they are studying. Technology is widely employed to explore notions and procedures related to more practical-operational subjects, whereas textbooks remain the main reference for more theoretical disciplines, possibly due to their ability to systematize and organise knowledge. However, when engaging in practical activities (exercises, research projects, theses), students consistently use digital resources and information. Some students reported exploring specialized channels to support university study, such as Docsity, an online platform for downloading study materials. Others use general social channels, particularly YouTube, to watch video lessons for understanding data analysis programs.

The type of device chosen to access these resources also impacts the time and place of study. The blend of 'real' and digital spaces, seen as environments of collective and connective knowledge, has reconfigured the learning process in terms of space, time, communication codes, and activities, as well as the identities of the actors – teacher and student – involved in a transformative process of skills, knowledge, and actions (Catone and Diana, 2019c).

For example, one group of respondents mentioned using digital content and tools to study directly from their mobile phones:

> I use it directly on the phone, almost never on the computer. Anyway, it's like doing everything on the phone, in the sense that the computer is even more inconvenient to carry, to open, it's even more boring maybe. On the other hand, the smartphone is much more immediate. (3F23)

> It is more feasible to use the mobile phone, you can read or listen to videos even on the bus with headphones. (9F22)

> During the day maybe, I don't have time to stay at home near the computer, I switch on the phone and see what I need, the information I simply need. (5M23)

Studying through digital resources and platforms seems to be on par with other internet activities; in other words, the generation of digital natives, who have grown up with digital languages, practices, and tools, use online resources anytime and anywhere. Thus, studying is increasingly detached from traditional space-time coordinates.

4.2 The blended learning experience

The second major dimension explored in focus groups concerns the blended learning experience in the Open Data course, specifically through the Google Classroom platform. The first aspect that emerged from discussions among interviewees is the platform's user-friendliness and how it provided students with real-time access to news, information, and communications, even if they did not regularly attend lessons.

> I notice the difference between when I enrolled in university and now... until a few years ago to receive news... for example, you had to check the noticeboard quite frequently for the exam date or other information, or some professor was communicating all the news...via the student associations but now with Google Classroom the news reaches everyone directly at the same time. (11F23)

You can always stay up to date, so you know what you must do. Those who don't have Google Classroom don't have the notification that, for example, you must deliver a certain task by tomorrow. (9M24)

Another important aspect for students was the ability to share and receive continuous feedback from their teacher or course mates on completed activities. The rapid evaluation of exercises and activities by both the teacher and other students through peer assessment plays a crucial role in developing critical and reflective skills. It enables learners to revisit underlying rules, internal criteria, and identify problems from multiple perspectives and unknown angles, fostering a mutual support network.

The written comments made by a professor or classmate during the activities almost in real-time also help us understand what is wrong and what is not. (6M23)

The peer assessment activities seemed more informal than the professor's assessment because they were done by a classmate and made the moment of assessment less rigid... then they invited me to reflect as I also had to evaluate and comment on the activities of other classmates and... in order to do this, I had to study in depth... (3F23)

In contrast to the survey results on the Social Research Methodology course, which highlighted low levels of socialization and collaboration, the Open Data for Social Research course emphasized the importance of relationships with teachers and classmates through various practices and activities. Unlike the previous methodology course, where individual learning prevailed, the Open Data course's activities had a strong collaborative component, which was particularly appreciated by the students.

Even with public comments...the professor may publish a post, and we can comment on it openly so that everyone can participate in the discussion. (9F22)

For example, in the past, we had to go to the Sociology website or the professor's website or exchange emails with the professor, which is a more cumbersome process, while on the platform everything is more immediate. (14F24)

Classroom is more like how you see it in class, in the email a tone of formality prevails because it is seen as something more formal, while maybe on Classroom that tone of formality is removed, and the communication is more direct. (6M23)

One group of interviewees noted that they implemented a more direct and immediate communication style, using informal language with their teacher.

From this perspective, the introduction of ICT could contribute to changing the educational relationship between teachers and students within "more liquid environments since it loses the typical space and time boundaries" (Capogna, 2017, p. 127). According to the focus group participants, the e-learning experience and the shared digital space contributed to a sense of belonging to the class. Students also believed that the course's success was due to the e-learning platform being integrated into in-class lessons, encouraging collaborative activities during lessons.

One key result that reflects the overall effectiveness of the course, especially the use of the platform for teaching concepts introduced in the Open Data for Social Research course, is that most students considered the platform a necessary channel for approaching tools and resources for empirical research methods in the digital context.

> It would have been much more difficult to understand the course contents by traditional means. Using this platform has also allowed us to implement the course effectively. Without this platform, we would have needed more hours of lessons. For example, the professor would share links on the platform for us to click on, but without the platform, maybe he would send them by email. (8M22)

> We did most activities in the classroom, but to do digital social research, we had to use a computer; the strong point is that the organised activities and resources of the platform allowed me not to get lost in the information overload of the Internet... to know which data to download, which database to access, which link to click to view the data. (15F24)

> It was possible to have an organised environment where you could know what to do, where to go, what tools to use... (14F24)

The e-learning environment, in addition to providing supporting tools and activities (external resources, forums, interactive exercises), acted as a direct channel that guided students, enabling them to understand the social research spaces available in the digital age.

> The external links inserted on the platform were useful to find out about the digital environments in which social research can be done... The various activities, especially collaborative ones, of the platform invited us to problematize the information contained in some platforms, learning by observing the structures and characteristics with which they are built. (6M23)

Social research spaces in the digital age can take on various meanings: as new contexts where individuals can share life experiences, developing social and interaction practices, and as environments structured according to different criteria in content organization, such as semantic fields (hashtags); temporal and spatial dimensions (universal timestamps, geotagging); and references (likes, shares; Wills 2016, p. 11). The "reinvention" of social research due to digital technologies involves not only "how" but also "where" (Snee et al. 2016), leading to significant methodological implications regarding the heterogeneity of elements characterizing these spaces.

> The activities proposed, for example, the qualitative observation of the platforms, led us to understand that the process of social research in the digital environment is more problematic, as we should try to understand or at least be aware that there are rules and choices underlying the placement and distribution of information... (8M22)

I emphasized to students the importance of reflecting on how devices impact and define conditions for producing social scientific knowledge. "Online social research is visibly a distributed accomplishment" (Marres, 2012, p. 160), and social research in digital environments involves practices and devices not of its own making, such as analytic measures embedded in online platforms (e.g., number of links, mentions, follower counts), and visual forms in visualisation modules (Marres, 2012, p. 160).

4.2.1 Interpretation and collaborative reporting

A further aspect concerns the blended learning experience, particularly the final phase of interpreting information and open data, which students considered complex. Often underestimated compared to advanced techniques for collecting and analysing digital information, data interpretation requires social researchers to give order and intelligibility to varied sets of heterogeneous traces and information, connecting them in a coherent meaning framework.

I aimed to enhance the value of interpretation by offering students the opportunity to produce a final report collaboratively, using resources from our teaching project. This final work required students to practice heuristic skills and place elements characterizing digital contexts in a sociological framework. Continuous interaction between student groups during the report completion and peer assessment moments built this interpretative ability. Creating a research project on a contemporary phenomenon using a critical and conscious approach to open data was appreciated by students, especially for understanding participatory and shared data visions and accessing public interest issues through specific social research paths.

Given the empirical research process's complexity in the digital context, especially in an advanced methodology course, the teacher's central role emerged, as students' opinions suggested:

Doing social research in the digital context requires collecting different types of information, and sometimes this phase is difficult; you get lost... there are many open data, collected with different procedures, in different years, referring to different units of analysis... learning to collect, analyse, and interpret them is possible only with someone guiding you to ask the right questions. So, a course like this done completely online... not, the teacher's presence is necessary because they ask you the right questions. (1F24)

In this course, the teacher, as a central guide on a problematic knowledge discovery path, enhanced collective and collaborative activity dimensions, understanding method as a choice – the ability or 'art' of making decisions case by case (Marradi, 1996), heuristic processes allowing new cognitive questions, and focusing on complex contexts (Barbera, 2006). Teachers helped students integrate and interpret the diverse elements characterizing digital environments within a broader framework.

4.2.2 Reflecting on the evaluation process

The results of the two didactic experiences using a blended learning model, along with previous research findings, have led us to carefully consider the multiple aspects necessary for quality e-learning. From our perspective, this means making choices free from technological automatisms, connected to students' needs, subject-matter peculiarities, and awareness of the risks of technologized knowledge and platformisation of education[2] in universities. Our empirical research results reiterate the central roles of teachers and students as key actors in this process. Teachers' roles proved fundamental throughout the educational path, helping to soften e-learning platforms' rigidity and personalize content, tools, and strategies. The two courses, linked by a common thread, underwent different design and implementation phases, translating into varied uses, experiences, and knowledge and skill development.

Finally, I considered students as crucial actors in building a reflective and collaborative process and an understanding space, enabling them to evolve

---

[2] The platformization of education refers to the integration and use of digital platforms and technologies for the delivery, management and enhancement of educational experiences. This includes the use of online tools and platforms to facilitate teaching, learning, assessment, and administration. Platformization is transforming traditional educational practices by enabling remote access to educational resources, promoting interactive and collaborative learning environments and allowing the collection and analysis of educational data. While it offers opportunities for innovation and flexibility in education, it also raises concerns about privacy, the quality of the learning experience, and potentially increasing dependence on technology.

from "consumers of quality to producers of quality" (Ghislandi and Raffaghelli, 2013, p. 273).

4.3 Significance and challenges of data visualisation in social research

Data visualisation refers to a set of analysis techniques used to represent the vast amount of information created daily and stored in various repositories (Friendly and Wainer, 2021). When coupled with a coherent data narrative, data visualisation assists the public (Diana and Ferrari, 2023; 2024), who often struggle to comprehend the complex dynamics of social crises, in making sense of uncertainty, assessing personal risk, and making informed decisions (Stone et al., 2015). Research indicates that information visualisation helps reduce mental load, enabling people to grasp transmitted content more quickly than through written text (Zhang, 2018).

The relevance of teaching and learning data visualisation has grown in academic training, particularly in social research methodology and digital methods for social research courses. Data visualisation is crucial in communicating and interpreting quantitative information, effectively representing complex social phenomena through graphs and interactive visualisations. In the digital age, where data is abundant (Big Data) and easily accessible (open data), the ability to create and interpret visualisations has become essential for social researchers and social science students. Data visualisation is especially important for developing social research projects in digital environments, where digital fieldwork is pivotal in data construction and narrative dissemination to specialist and non-specialist audiences (Selwyn, 2019; Marres, 2017; Lupton, 2014). The advent of Big Data and new data processing technologies has granted a wider audience of professionals and laypeople access to previously inaccessible quantitative information (Risi, 2022; Veltri, 2019; Marres, 2017; Lupton, 2014).

Despite its growing importance, teaching data visualisation presents significant challenges. Academic literature highlights the need to balance practical training with a strong theoretical understanding of data visualisation, with the ethical aspects of data representation often being underestimated. These issues question the effectiveness of traditional approaches to teaching data visualisation in social research methodology courses. This second empirical study aimed to examine the teaching and learning experience of data visualisation within the Digital Methods for Social Research course at the University of Salerno during the 2022/2023 academic year. Specific objectives included analysing students' reactions and challenges during lectures and lab activities, exploring learning strategies adopted by students, highlighting the ethical aspects of data analysis and manipulation, collecting student feedback, and identifying obstacles to learning and areas for improvement.

An ethnographic approach was used to achieve these objectives, allowing for an in-depth exploration of students' experiences and perspectives within the course context.

Data visualisation is a practice that involves the graphical representation of complex data to make information more understandable, accessible, and useful (Ryan et al., 2019). This process of translating data into visual elements such as charts, diagrams, maps, and more facilitates the communication of trends, relationships, and patterns present in the data. But data visualisation goes beyond simply creating charts; it involves the careful selection of visual representations and the ability to interpret these representations. In social research, data visualisation plays a crucial role. The data collected in social science research often encompasses a wide range of complex information, including demographic data, opinions, behaviours, social interactions, and more. A fundamental element of data visualisation is the ability to transform "raw data" into coherent visual narratives (storytelling). This visual narrative is essential to engage the audience, often composed of non-specialists, in understanding complex data and making informed decisions. Despite a promising start, sociology has lagged in the use of visual tools (Healy and Moody, 2014). Yet, data visualisation has proven essential not only for presenting data (Tufte, 1990) but also for analysing it (Friendly and Wainer, 2021; Engebretsen and Kennedy, 2020). With the rapid increase in data visualisation tools (e.g., Google Trends, GapMinder, ManyEyes, Tableau) and the rise of graphics in the media, understanding the principles of good graphics and the ability to create effective visualisations have become increasingly important aspects of training sociologists and social researchers (Nolan and Perrett, 2016). Most texts explain how to present data based on their nature, how to adapt presentations to different types of audiences, or focus on ethical criteria (Wolfe, 2015), but they do not consider the interpretative level, which is fundamental in choosing between competing and equally valid interpretations (Perelman and Olbrechts-Tyteca, 1969). The rhetorical and creative nature of data interpretation is often underestimated, especially at the pedagogical level, and is almost never explained and even less applied. In university and post-graduate education, integrating the teaching of data visualisation within digital methods courses offers students a unique opportunity to develop so-called "reflexivity" (Schön, 1987; 1983) and, consequently, the critical skills necessary for social research (Lupton, 2015). However, it is important to consider the appropriate pedagogical approach to maximise student learning and promote their competence in creating and interpreting data visualisations.

4.3.1 Teaching and pedagogical methodology

The teaching approach used in the course is based on a constructivist assumption (Catone and Diana, 2020; Diana and Catone, 2018; Catone and Diana, 2017;

Rossi, 2010; Lave and Wenger, 2006; Wenger, 1999; Calvani, 1998). According to this perspective, students are active participants in the learning process, constructing meanings and knowledge through interaction with content, classmates, and the learning environment. The constructivist approach emphasizes active student engagement, critical thinking, and problem-solving. In the context of data visualisation, the constructivist approach allows students to become co-creators of their knowledge rather than passive spectators. From the beginning of the course, students were encouraged to explore, experiment, and create data visualisations independently, significantly contributing to their learning process. Several pedagogical strategies were implemented in the course to facilitate learning data visualisation techniques. First, students were introduced to the principles of data visualisation. They gained a theoretical understanding of the basic principles of data visualisation, including graph types, visual design principles, the use of colours and symbols, data presentation clarity, and best practices for data representation. This theoretical approach provided them with a critical understanding of visualisation choices.

The ethical aspect of data visualisation was emphasized during the course. Students examined the ethical implications of data selection, manipulation, and presentation, recognizing the importance of accurate and responsible information representation to avoid social issues such as the proliferation of fake news and the instrumental manipulation of data for partisan interests. Problem-solving-based learning was also a key strategy. Students faced real-world challenges and problems that required the use of data visualisation tools to be solved. This approach motivated them to seek creative solutions and develop practical skills. Group work was encouraged through collaborative learning activities. Students worked together in creating and analysing data visualisations, learning from each other's collaboration.

The course provided access and training on software dedicated to data visualisation. Initially, an introduction to the basic functionalities of Excel and how to manage data in a "*CxV*" (Cases x Variables) table was given, and later, participants were provided with the tools and resources necessary to create effective data visualisations, with a particular emphasis on using Tableau software. Students learned to upload, process, and represent data interactively, acquiring practical skills in creating professional visualisations.

Practical projects and final work were integral to the course. Students participated in numerous practical projects and exercises that stimulated them to create data visualisations based on real data extracted from the web. These projects were an opportunity to apply theoretical knowledge to practice and develop skills in visual communication, culminating in group work where five groups of three students each were involved in creating a project of data analysis and visualisation using Tableau on six different case studies (*Table 4.1*) chosen by the instructor (the *Iran case*, the *Egonu case*, the *Paralympics case*, the *World Cup case*, the *Butterflies case*, the *Social University case*). The group work involved data extraction from social media platforms, with the help of a social media listening platform (Blogmeter), to which students had access thanks to the involvement during an expert in political communication and social media analysis, who intervened twice during the course to demonstrate the use of some of these social media listening platforms. These were then kindly and freely provided to the students attending the course for a week, allowing them time to research their assigned case study and extract data, observing the trends and interactions over seven days.

Table 4.1. Summary table of the main characteristics of the students' final group projects presented on December 5, 2022.

Teamwork	No. Students	Case Study	Title	Scraping Software	Social Media Analysed	Time Frame Considered	Analysis Technique	Data Visualisation Software	Type of Visualisation
A	2	Iran	Iran: An investigation on current events	Blogmeter	Twitter	Last 7 months	Secondary data analysis, frequency and occurrence analysis	Tableau, Tableau Public, Statista, Google trends, Live gap charts	Map chart, pie chart, bar chart
B	2	Paola Egonu	Paolo Egonu: Every medal has two sides	Blogmeter	Instagram, Facebook, YouTube, Twitter	October 13-20, 2022	Sentiment analysis, network analysis	Tableau, Netlytic, Excel, Word art	Line chart, map chart, table, pie chart, bubbles, tree chart, bar chart, word cloud, network analysis
C	2	Paralympics	Paralympics Report	Blogmeter	Twitter, News, Blog, Forum, Instagram, YouTube, Reddit, TikTok	March 4-13, 2022, last 12 months (2021-2022)	Sentiment analysis	Tableau	Line chart, bubbles, stacked bar chart, histogram
D	2	Football World Cup	Football World Cup	Blogmeter	Twitter, News, Blog, Forum, Instagram, YouTube, Reddit, TikTok	Last 12 months (2021-2022)	Sentiment analysis	Tableau	Pie chart, word cloud, line chart, stacked bar chart
E	2	Butterflies	Rhythmic Gymnastics: Body shaming among the Butterflies	Blogmeter	Instagram, Facebook	Last 3 months	Sentiment analysis	Tableau	Line chart, histogram
F	2	Social Universities	The most social Italian universities	Blogmeter	Instagram, Facebook, YouTube, Twitter, TikTok, LinkedIn, Flickr	Last 3 months	Content analysis	Tableau, Excel	Word cloud, map chart, bar chart, bubbles, table, histogram, pie chart, tree chart

The results of teaching and learning data visualisation were evaluated through various means, including exams, practical projects, and ongoing classroom feedback through discussions and comparisons with the instructor. Most students demonstrated significant growth in their skills, particularly in the following areas: the ability to create effective data visualisations (*Table 4.2*). Students were assessed on their ability to create effective data visualisations. They demonstrated the ability to select appropriate charts and representations for the provided data, use colours and symbols consistently, and create clear and understandable visualisations. Practical project examples showed their ability to apply these skills in real contexts using Excel and Tableau (Tableau Desktop) and communicate and share results through classroom presentations and sharing operations on Tableau's dedicated platforms for sharing research projects (Tableau Public and Tableau Cloud).

Table 4.2. Frequency of use of different types of data visualisation in the students' final group projects presented on December 5, 2022.

Teamwork	Case study	Map chart	Pie chart	Line chart	Table	Bubbles	Three chart	Word cloud	Histogram	Bar chart	Stacked Bar chart	Network analysis	TOTAL
A	Iran	3	1	2	0	0	0	0	2	2	0	0	10
B	Paola Egonu	1	1	3	1	1	1	1	0	1	0	1	11
C	Paralympics	0	0	4	0	2	0	0	0	7	2	0	15
D	Football World Cup	0	3	3	0	0	0	1	0	0	2	0	9
E	Butterflies	0	0	1	0	0	0	0	0	4	0	0	5
F	Social Universities	1	1	0	1	1	1	1	0	4	0	0	10
TOTAL		5	6	13	2	4	2	3	2	18	4	1	60

Another crucial aspect of learning was the students' ability to interpret data visualisations created by others. This included analysing the validity of visualisations, detecting possible biases, and understanding the narratives (storytelling, "stories" in Tableau language) that the data tell through visual representations. Students were also exposed to a variety of data visualisation examples during the course and participated in critical discussions about their interpretation during the theoretical part of the course.

The results of our research indicate that integrating this skill more generally into methodology and social research technique courses is highly recommended and fruitful for students, representing an important asset for building the "toolbox" that every good social analyst should have and for forming a background that can count in post-university careers. During the course, students demonstrated the ability to create effective visualisations and critically interpret those created by others. These skills are essential for their training as social researchers and experts in the job market, in an era where digital data is omnipresent and visual communication is fundamental for understanding and persuading large audiences. However, some issues emerged during the learning process. It was noted that although students acquired practical skills in data visualisation, it is important to further develop their critical ability in evaluating visualisations and identifying possible biases or distortions. Additionally, theoretical training is essential to ensure that students fully understand the principles behind data visualisation and the ethical implications of their practice.

4.4 Ethnographic approach and participant observation[3]

To gain an in-depth understanding of data visualisation learning and course dynamics, an ethnographic approach was used. Ethnography is a qualitative research methodology that aims to understand the behaviours, cultures, and practices of a group or community through participant observation and direct interaction with participants. Participant observation was a key component of the ethnographic approach. The researcher/instructor actively participated in the course lessons, laboratory activities, email exchanges, and class discussions, acting as a participant observer. This allowed him to gain a direct perspective on students' experiences during the course, including the challenges faced and learning strategies adopted. During participant observation, detailed ethnographic notes were taken, and relevant observations were recorded about students' interactions, their reactions to educational activities, and course dynamics. These observations were then analysed to identify significant patterns and trends.

One of the main problems that emerged from the beginning of the course was the inadequacy of students' computers: low-quality machines that, especially at the start, did not allow for fluid transitions in the main steps of acquiring Excel and Tableau functionalities. Additionally, working in a lab equipped with high-performing computers with the software already installed and functioning would certainly speed up the initial phases of the course, where a lot of time is usually lost downloading and installing the software; however, it does not allow students to work fully independently, especially in the study and knowledge consolidation phase at home. This problem could be overcome by providing students with high-performing laptops with all the necessary software installed at the beginning of their course, which can be returned to the lab or department after completing the course and passing the exam.

---

[3] In the Appendix of this book, the reader will find various examples of data visualisations from the students' final projects.

In group work, other difficulties emerged, particularly in adapting individuals to work in teams. This is due to various reasons, the main one being the nature of Italian public universities, which still do not integrate theory and practice, often offering a type of teaching and learning solely focused on information assimilation and a discursive approach, which favours individualistic study over sharing and collaboration with other students. Additionally, students were observed to be unprepared in basic computer use, specifically in using Excel and online material sharing functionalities. This aspect should be addressed much earlier in academic training.

Another critical issue observed from the class's group dynamics was the latent need for the instructor to create a "community of practice" (Fabbri, 2007; Wenger, 1999) that facilitates learning through sharing a common goal. This process encountered various difficulties and obstacles from students, hindered by an at times excessive resistance to technology as a whole and its manifestations, almost reflected in a fear expressed in immobility in front of unknown software (Tableau), producing a paralysis in front of the screen instead of experimentation mechanisms through trial and error. Specifically, for the final projects presented by students in pairs at the end of the course (December 5, 2022), two summary tables were drawn up and included among the Attachments to this document: The first is a summary table of the main characteristics of the students' final group projects; The second table reports the frequency of use of different types of data visualisation in the students' final group projects. The first table contains specific information about the students' final group projects: the six assigned case studies, the title given by the students to their presentation, the scraping software used for data extraction, the social media analysed, the time frame considered in the analysis, the data analysis techniques used, the data visualisation software used, and the types of data visualisation adopted. The second table shows that a total of 11 different types of data visualisation were used in the six presentations (map chart, pie chart, line chart, table, bubbles, tree chart, word cloud, histogram, bar chart, stacked bar chart, and network analysis). It also highlights that some types of data visualisation covered extensively during the course were not used in any presentation (heat map, scatter plot, area chart). A total of 60 data elaborations were produced using these 11 types of data visualisation mentioned above, with the most used types being bar chart (18) and line chart (13), while the least used were network analysis (1), tree chart (2), table (2), and histogram (2), with an average of ten elaborations per each of the six presentations. Lastly, it also indicates the maturation of certain autonomy and reflexivity by students in using work tools, but also in the theoretical elaboration of their final works, evidenced by the appropriation and use of Tableau Public resources, Tableau's free platform for exploring, creating, and sharing data visualisations online. The table also indicates use of other devices and applications like Netlytic, introduced in another part of the course, or different research techniques to perform data analysis: sentiment analysis (4), content analysis (1), network analysis (1), secondary data analysis (1), frequency and occurrence analysis (1)[4].

The research results provided a detailed view of the data visualisation learning experience in the course. Several significant themes and considerations emerged:

- Challenges in learning: Students faced challenges in understanding the theoretical concepts of data visualisation and using the software. Some reported the need for additional resources to deepen their understanding and more lab hours to have more time to practice in class and acquire practical skills using the software presented during the course.

- Variations in approach: Students adopted different attitudes towards learning data visualisation. Some focused on the practical aspect, while others emphasized theory more. This highlighted the diversity of student learning modes.

- Positive feedback on the course: Overall, students expressed positive feedback on the course and appreciated the practical, problem-solving-based approach. They recognized the value of the skills acquired in data visualisation for their training and future careers.

- Suggestions for improving teaching: Students provided suggestions for improving the course, including greater emphasis on theoretical training, additional resources for autonomous learning, preliminary basic training, especially in basic statistics and Excel use, and more hours dedicated to lab practice.

Beyond traditional ethical considerations related to informed consent, confidentiality, and researcher positionality, digital ethnography must now operate within an increasingly complex regulatory framework. In particular, two recent European regulations – the General Data Protection Regulation (GDPR) and the Digital Services Act (DSA) – have introduced new challenges that directly affect how researchers design, conduct, and report digital social research.

The GDPR (European Parliament and Council, 2016) imposes strict requirements on data collection and processing, especially when data may be linked to identifiable individuals. Researchers must ensure data minimization, purpose limitation, and lawful processing, typically through explicit, informed consent. Even in digital spaces where data appears "public," such as forums or social

---

[4] Some examples of the visualizations created by the students for their final group projects are provided in the Appendix.

media, GDPR principles often apply due to the potential identifiability of user traces (Zimmer and Kinder-Kurlanda, 2017).

Meanwhile, the DSA (European Commission, 2022) primarily targets the responsibilities of digital platforms, but it also affects researchers indirectly. The DSA introduces transparency obligations, particularly around automated content moderation, algorithmic ranking, and access to platform data. Researchers relying on scraped data or public APIs must consider the legality and terms of access under this new framework and be prepared for shifting availability or restrictions (Markham and Buchanan, 2012).

Together, these developments call for a more compliance-aware and reflexive research practice. Navigating the ethical-legal terrain of digital research today often requires interdisciplinary collaboration, for instance, with legal experts or institutional data protection officers, to ensure both methodological rigor and regulatory alignment.

Chapter 5
Narrative in social research: Tradition and innovation

5.1 The evolution of narrative in social sciences

In the last few decades, there has been growing interest in approaches to narrative in the human and social sciences (Riessman, 1993; Somers, 1994; Mishler, 1995; Czarniawska, 2004). In the mid-1980s, in fact, a renewed interest in a multiplicity of models of knowledge that recognize the interpretative methods, uses and functions of rhetoric in scientific research and the potential and value of narratives (Bonet, 2005) led to the 'narrative turn' (Riessman, 2008). In the period preceding the 'narrative turn' – a period marked by the passage from modernity to the post-modern era and a decline in the absolute and objective conception of science – many scholars in fact contributed to the development of narratives not only in social research but also in the natural sciences (Bonet, 2005).

Dilthey, for example, dealt with the scientific status of history; Max Weber focused on the interpretative process of social action; and Alfred Schütz highlighted the role of the relationship between action and forms of symbolic mediation, arguing that meanings as socially constructed are the result of personal interactions and conversations.

According to Hyvärinen (2016), the pre-history of narrative sociology was mainly focused on the biographical tradition, i.e., the use of narratives as research materials. Hence, in *The Polish Peasant in Europe and America*, Thomas and Znaniecki's (1984) collected letters from immigrants as source material for sociological analysis, reversing the behaviourist paradigm and underlining the difference in attitudes and values in social action. Within the tradition of the Chicago school, life stories were a technique used by Shaw; Jerome Bruner then introduced two forms of thought, comparing knowledge deriving from the narrative mode with that from the logico-scientific mode; and Paul Ricoeur explored the relationship between temporality and narrative through phenomenological theory.

An increasing interest in language during that period, together with the diffusion of social constructionist ideas and the development of qualitative research, created a context in which the narrative turn began to develop: a deeper, more specific interest in narrative in the social sciences that can be found in the edited *Biography and Society collection* by Daniel Bertaux (1981) and Elliot Mishler's book, *Research Interviewing: Context and Narrative* (1986).

Starting from this context, this article aims to provide an overview of the role of narratives for sociological analysis from both a theoretical and a methodological point of view.

The first section, through an analysis of the main characteristics of the narrative process, explores how narrative allows sociologists to understand the increasing complexity of everyday life in our contemporary, technological society, in which common sense and identity are closely interconnected. The second section deals with the role of narrative in social research: Having analysed the main methods that use narrative to understand everyday life, we identify the key characteristics and the similarities and differences between traditional and emerging techniques. These new techniques are connected to the increase in the use of digital devices and to the so-called 'data deluge,' which has led to changes in the implementation of empirical research.

In the final section, we illustrate how digital technology could open up new possibilities in the field of narrative in empirical research. By adopting the distinction provided by Richard Rogers (2013) between the 'digitization' of methods and 'natively digital' methods, we examine some features of the emerging techniques aimed at analysing the narratives embedded within multiple aspects of everyday life, narrated by contemporary individuals within new digital environments.

5.2 The role of narrative in analysing contemporary everyday life

Narrative has been the subject of several – at times controversial – definitions and analytical approaches. Before starting an analysis of these, it is necessary to make some distinctions between terms such as the 'story', 'tale' and 'narration,' which are usually considered synonymous, but which refer to three distinct concepts. While the first concerns the events that are the subject of a certain discourse and the second covers the discourse in itself – i.e. the statement through which a certain set of events is communicated – narrative refers to the act of telling, meaning the act by which in a given situation, someone tells something to another (Jedlowski, 2000).

In general,

> a narrative can be understood to organise a sequence of events into a whole so that the significance of each event can be understood through its relation to that whole. In this way a narrative conveys the meaning of events (Elliot, 2005, p. 3).

This definition encapsulates three interconnected aspects that underline the value of narrative within sociology (Elliot, 2005).

The first aspect is that of the temporal dimension, since the narrative represents a sequence of events. Time is a fundamental variable for understanding social action, as it is itself embedded in time, and understanding time is narrating (Jedlowski, 2000).

From the perspective of the individuals involved at the centre of the analysis, narrative can foster empathy in an individual who "can externalize his or her feelings and indicate which elements of those experiences are most significant" (Elliot, 2005, p. 3). According to this approach,

> narrative is a meaning structure that organises events and human actions into a whole, thereby attributing significance to individual actions and events according to their effect on the whole (Polkinghorne, 1988, p. 18).

Considering the ideographic dimension – that relies on the richness and depth of the singularity and not on generalization – narratives allow the person to organise the world from their own point of view, providing connections and patterns of interpretation. These patterns are a way for them to reaffirm and construct their own identity through a narrative (Bichi, 2000). In this regard, according to Somers (1994), the meaning of the events characterizing a narrative is not given by their chronological order but is provided by an "emplotment" that "allows us to construct a significant network or configuration of relationships" (Somers, 1994, p. 617).

The third aspect involves the social nature of narrative, given that it is produced for a specific audience and within a specific social context. According to Poggio (2004), narration is a form of social interaction for several reasons:

- It does not take place in a vacuum but happens within a communicative and transitive interaction that implies an interlocutor. In other words, it establishes a connection with one or more recipients and a negotiation of the agreement on what is narrated. More specifically, a narrative moves within a dynamic and relational discourse which follows two main directions: a) 'to ourselves', as the narrator's discourses and descriptions contribute to the construction of their identity; b) 'to significant others', i.e., the recipients of the communication, situated in a specific field of action for which the narrator believes that the construction of that specific detail is significant (Melucci, 1996).

- It is deeply connected to the use of language, i.e., a dialogical construct based on the human relationship. Hence, the social world is inconceivable without the mediation of language because it orients and orders the meanings (Montesperelli, 2017).

- It is a social construction that connects events by giving them meaning. Narrative can therefore be considered as an interpretative process, i.e., the result of a world of shared and situated meanings (Jedlowski, 2000). This means that narrating is never a neutral action that is independent from the identity of the person who is narrating, from their motivations, or from the context in which the narration takes place (Bichi, 2000, p. 58). In other words, narratives are situated in a framework that is constructed by several subjects, objects, and actions that are part of the social world of the subject themselves (Connelly and Clandinin, 2007); they represent the basis of our collective imaginary, i.e., the set of tacit knowledge that we usually share with all the members of the groups to which we belong, and that allows us to live together (Pecchinenda, 2009).

In short, we can say that a narrative identifies a connection of events which follow a chronological, logical, and argumentative sequence (Atkinson, 1998). More specifically, narratives can be conceived as constellations of relationships embedded in time and space and constituted by a causal 'emplotment' (Somers, 1994, p. 617). This means that narrations allow the subject to identify the causes and motivations, selecting and connecting the events and actions in a causal relationship, i.e., reconnecting them to a logically coherent structure. From this perspective, the cognitive dimension of narratives is found in this ability to find meaning in everything that is disconnected and inhomogeneous (Longo, 2012; 2017).

All these characteristics have made narrative central to sociological analysis. Narration is indeed the main form of human communication (Bichi, 2000) and a person is a "*homo loquens*" (Longo, 2005) because of their natural tendency to narrate aspects of their own being and their own life (Longo, 2005), representing and giving meaning to experiences in the form of a narrative. The opportunity to narrate also has a direct relationship with identity (Montesperelli, 1998): "We come to know, understand, and make sense of the social world, and it is through narratives and narrativity that we constitute our social identities" (Somers, 1994, p. 606). In this regard, Somers (1994) introduced the concepts of ontological narratives, i.e., the stories that social actors use to define who they are.

Another aspect of the connection between sociology and narratives is provided by their contributions both to developing social bonds and to building shared interpretations of reality. Sociology focuses specifically on these two dimensions: first, as actions embedded in social relations, and second, as a means of accessing the ways in which subjects attribute meaning to their own reality.

The interest of sociologists in narratives is also a result of the awareness that they are part of everyday life. They mark time, build meaning, and foster memory (Poggio, 2004), and thus they can allow social researchers to gain a better understanding of the context. The world of everyday life – i.e., the internalized experience that encompasses common sense – allows for social interaction and fosters the sense of mutual belonging (Montesperelli, 1998); it is constantly marked by the stories that we create every day. Moreover, given that everyday life is characterized by a common sense that is the result of a social construction, most narratives can be conceived as the way in which this construction is realised (Schütz, 1967; Jedlowski, 2000).

The analysis of narrative to explore the world of everyday life acquires a specific meaning when contextualized in contemporary society, which, due to its increasing complexity, needs to be read starting from the significant fragments of reality from these everyday stories (Longo, 2017).

The society we live in today is a narrative moment (Maines, 1993), since the contemporary individual has the tendency and the need to express themselves and communicate their actions, feelings, and opinions in a multiplicity of ways. He or she is a subject who shares their feelings to affirm their own identity and contribute to the collective conversation (Lupton, 2014). This is because the development of the Internet and ICT has opened up new channels through which individuals express the narratives of their everyday lives (Romney, Johnson and Roschke, 2017; Thumim, 2009), writing status updates, commenting, liking content, and posting photos. People often use the opportunities provided by the web to construct their own narratives, to talk about themselves and reflect on their actions and opinions (Bennato, 2015). The world of blogs, social networks (e.g., Facebook, Twitter, Storify), forums, etc., shows us an environment of media culture that revolves around the individual and collective narrative (Boccia Artieri, 2012). Within these environments, individuals are used to expressing symbolic artefacts, events, and activities and to textualizing and visualizing their life in a digital form, through narrative.

The Internet is thus deeply connected with our habits and becomes a space where our opinions and news develop dynamically. This has an impact on the representation of our identity, which can be conceived as the visible product of our connections and input (Boccia Artieri, 2012). This complex and multifaceted configuration gives rise to the need to investigate the narratives underpinning the digital society and highlights the importance of identifying appropriate methods and tools to address their analysis and interpretation. As Deborah Lupton argues, "the investigating of our interactions with digital technologies contributes to research into the nature of human experience, it also tells us much about the social world" (Lupton, 2014, p. 2).

The use of narratives in empirical research generally falls within the qualitative approach, based on the centrality of individuals and aimed at understanding these phenomena, their subjective meanings, and the contexts in which they are generated. Based on these assumptions, life stories, in-depth interviews, case studies, and ethnographic observations have been the traditional qualitative techniques used to explore the social experience of the narrators, to understand the social world of which they are members (Bichi, 2000), and to reveal the world of meanings in all its complexity. However, as will be seen in the following sections, the need to adopt a narrative approach also in the analysis of digital contexts is opening new theoretical and methodological issues and challenges that have different peculiarities from those traditionally recognized in the methodological literature. These narratives, which are developed in the digital context, weave together images, texts, and videos, and hence call for specific techniques and tools capable of interpreting the complex nature of multimedia and interactivity.

5.3 Narrative approaches in social research

In the previous section, we examined how narrative acts as an important cognitive tool that can be adopted in sociology to explore the world of everyday life, conceived as the intersubjective world of meanings. It is through the form of reality construction provided by narrative that it is possible to understand the peculiarities and changes taking place in the world in which we live. Narrative allows us to reconstruct a story of the subject within the stories of others along the dimensions of space and time; it provides an interpretation of events, practices, and experiences, giving meaning to what is considered significant for the subject (Besozzi and Colombo, 2014). As Bruner claims (1986), the narrative approach, in contrast to logical thinking based on a formal apparatus of representation of reality, which is considered objective and external, develops and connects a set of events with social and relational contents (Besozzi and Colombo, 2014).

According to Longo (2005), most social research methods are based on the narratives collected by the researcher. Depending on the cognitive aim of the research, the researcher can either use them as a source of data to be generalized (in the case of quantitative techniques) or consider them in their uniqueness in order to identify the connections that link the biographical and social dimensions (in the case of qualitative techniques).

More specifically, among the different techniques that focus on narrative, one of the most common ways to collect stories is to stimulate and solicit them through the interview (Poggio, 2004; Marradi, 2005; Addeo and Diana, 2010).

Considered in its different meanings as a dialogue (Guidicini, 1968) – a conversation with a specific aim (Bingham and Moore, 1924) – the interview is an interaction between two or more subjects aimed at providing relevant information on a cognitive object for research purposes (Tusini, 2006).

As highlighted by Addeo and Montesperelli (2007), the common aspect underlying these different definitions concerns the relational nature of the interview, as it is a form of social interaction or conversation undertaken by two or more people. In their view, an interview can be considered as a specialized form of communication in which several people engage in verbal and non-verbal interaction to achieve a cognitive goal (Fideli and Marradi, 1996).

In methodological literature, interview techniques can be classified into structured, semi-structured, and unstructured according to the three different criteria of structuring, standardization, and directivity (Corbetta, 2003; Bichi, 2005). While the structured interview provides the interviewees with a limited opportunity to express themselves (since the same questions are asked to all the interviewees in the same order so that the answers can be compared and analysed for statistical purposes), the semi-structured and unstructured interviews aim at understanding and constructing intersubjective representations, so both the interviewer and the interviewee have more freedom to interact and communicate with each other.

It is within the unstructured interview that narrative practice is generated, as a deeper level of interaction is developed between the interviewee and the interviewer. These types of interviews are non-directive techniques – part of the broader family of qualitative methods – that allow the researcher to understand the world of everyday life, the point of view of the subject and their peculiarities through a flexible approach tailored to each subject (Diana and Montesperelli, 2005).

In these types of techniques, the interviewer, starting with the introduction of the main theme of the research, leaves the respondent free to answer by expressing themselves using verbal and nonverbal codes (Pitrone, 2009). This is because the cognitive aim behind the interview is to reach an understanding of the everyday life of the subject who, following the principle of the centrality of the respondent, is the true expert of the context in which they live, and thus of their own biography (Diana and Montesperelli, 2005). In this way, the narrative dimension of an unstructured interview lies in the opportunity given to the interviewee to narrate their life using their own language, activating a process of (re)construction of their personal experiences and of their social identity. An interview about the world of everyday life can represent a particular encouragement to narrate, to reconstruct one's own identity (Montesperelli, 1998), and to give voice to everything that cannot be detected with standardized techniques. Especially in some types of non-directive techniques, such as the hermeneutic interview, the phenomena to be analysed can be closely assimilated to the narrative text, giving rise to some important implications on the side of the narrator: their identity is formed narratively, through the ability to reflect on their life, to establish a narrative continuity between their different experiences. Through narrative, the interviewee makes experiences and events which would otherwise be too heterogeneous and meaningless, organised, and intelligible (Montesperelli, 1998).

An important aspect of this type of interview relates to the interaction between the interviewer and the interviewee, which at times recalls the communicative processes of everyday life conversations (Addeo and Montesperelli, 2007). However, it should be remembered that the interview situation is artificial because it cannot be conceived as "a natural reflection of the real conditions outside the field of research" (Roulston, 2010). The interview is a different situation from true conversation: in contrast to spontaneous everyday life conversations, the interview, the aim of which is to pursue a cognitive goal, takes place in a research context (Fideli and Marradi, 1996). Moreover, since the situation is artificial (i.e., specifically created for scientific aims and characterized by the presence of an interviewer), this can generate a series of distortions, such as social desirability.

Another important issue that makes the interview different from other forms of social interaction concerns the relationship between the interviewer and the interviewee. This usually takes on an asymmetrical format, as it is the interviewer who stimulates the respondent to answer (Addeo and Montesperelli, 2007). Clearly, non-directive techniques partly reduce this asymmetry as the interviewer has the task of creating a condition of listening to put the interviewee at the centre of the interaction. In this way, through an in-depth interpretative process, the interviewer tries to grasp all the peculiarities of the verbal and non-verbal language that is used during the narration.

As anticipated in the previous section, the so-called *homo loquens* (Longo, 2017), in contemporary digital society expresses themselves and their experiences in a multiplicity of ways and channels that generate new scenarios in the social sciences, both on a theoretical and a methodological level. Digital technology in fact opens up many possibilities in the field of narrative (Given, 2006), due to the rise in user participation in the creation of online content. It is now common for individuals to report on their own everyday lives, sharing and commenting on their experiences (Marres, 2017). The increasingly pervasive use of the Internet makes it a phenomenon embedded in multiple contexts of everyday life (Roberts et al., 2016). The use of wearables – devices that allow the subject to be permanently connected to the web – is one example of this pattern. In other words, the sociologist today has to deal with a multiplicity of sources, from which it is possible to trace narrations and interpret their meanings. This is because the contemporary subject crosses, with extreme rapidity and ease of access, more "finite provinces of meaning" (Schütz, 1967; Bennato, 2012) than in the past.

When the narrative is expressed in a digital context, the nature of the data (text, image, video, etc.) and the whole design of the research can radically change (Given, 2006). First of all, the interlocutor (i.e., the user) to whom the subject addresses their narrative, is not the interviewer or the researcher, but the sometimes-blurred mass of people who inhabit the web. There is, therefore, a significant transformation in the nature of the narrative relationship, moving from "one to one," to a potential "one to many." This change, in fact, has an influence on a great many aspects.

In contrast to an interview, in which the subject is asked and urged by the interviewer to narrate in a specific and predefined research situation, in the digital context the subject narrates more naturally and without any interference.

As stated by Noortje Marres (2017), the information provided by digital infrastructures are not the 'designed' data that are usually collected by traditional research methods and that are characterized as 'single purpose,' i.e., for a scientific aim. Instead, digital media technologies allow us to access and analyse different types of unsolicited materials, such as text, photos, videos, tags, and so on (Robinson, 2001), that are produced 'naturally' as part of social life. Hence, most of the data of digital platforms, being 'naturally occurring,' user-generated contents, are already available, thereby addressing a recognized, methodological problem related to the 'artificial quality' of the data (Marres, 2017).

Within the debate on the naturalness of digital data, Marres also recalls the doubts expressed by some sociologists who state that "platform-based and other forms of digital data are formatted in ways that agree with specific social methods, such as network analysis and conversation analysis" (Marres, 2017, p. 46). From this perspective, "online data is not 'natural' data, insofar as digital content and digital action is often highly formatted" (Marres, 2017, p. 46). Another issue relates to the concept of 'data' itself, that in the digital context can be configured in a variety of ways. On this subject, Bruno Latour and others (2012) adopted the term 'trace': While data implies a specific architecture, such as the database, the trace is more minimal and maintains a reference to the device from which it was detected (Marres and Weltevrede, 2013; Marres, 2017).

The absence of the researcher/interviewer leads to other differences from the face-to-face research setting: the subject may feel freer to express themselves, revealing things that they would not discuss in a traditional interview context (Seale et al., 2010). This means that the digital context could potentially be conceived as a tool for exploring more sensitive topics that are often hard to discuss using traditional face-to-face techniques (Seale et al., 2010; Lee, 1993). Moreover, according to Seale et al. (2010, p. 596), Internet communications might change the factors that in face-to-face situations result in a particular performance of an idealized self, or "front." Of course, also on the Internet, the narrations must be interpreted in the light of distortions such as social desirability, connected to specific strategies for visibility of the users (Boccia Artieri et al., 2018; Zywica and Danowski, 2008).

However, an important issue of investigation in a digital environment is the impossibility of being able to grasp all the non-verbal aspects of communication that represent a fundamental cognitive source supporting narration: the para-linguistic aspects, for example (the intonation and the volume of the voice, the accents, the rhythm and the speed of the speech, the use of the pauses, etc.); mimicking (body movements, gestures, facial expressions etc.); and proxemics (the placement of the respondent in the space etc.; Addeo and Montesperelli, 2007). This information, that allows us to understand the communication process in its complexity and entirety, is lacking in the digital artefacts. But it is not only the lack of non-verbal signals that can have an impact, but also the absence of the interviewer, which could, on the one hand, favour a greater freedom of expression in the subject narrating. On the other hand, however, it implies renouncing the hermeneutic sensibility, the 'art of listening,' the empathy that allows the subject to reconstruct their most significant experiences.

The interviewer is therefore a fundamental figure who facilitates an in-depth exploration of specific issues employing a cooperative approach, hence avoiding certain distortions. Moreover, the entire interview process, considered as a verbal interaction that is missing in the Internet environment, can also stimulate reflection (Montesperelli, 1998). Another important question concerns the type of narrative message produced on the web: it can be a social network post, an image, a photo, a video, an article on a blog, or a message on a discussion forum. While the information collected through the non-directive techniques, however polysemic, is characterized by a certain unitarity giving a valid empirical basis within which the researcher can move, the information collected on the web is various and unstructured. This requires the researcher to reconstruct the horizon of meaning that binds these elements together, as well as giving rise to the need to tackle the complex methodological issues that represent the new frontiers of social research.

These aspects make us reflect on the meaning of digital narratives. In fact, although the empirical basis of these is richer and more accessible, they also raise important questions regarding the interpretative process that must be implemented by the researcher.

The naturalness of digital data poses a series of questions regarding the interpretation of the narrative act in the sphere of its meaning, something that is given intentionally by the subject. For example, in the "one to many" communication that often characterizes the Internet environment, reconstructing the cognitive framework that includes a common sense, culture, and a values system through which to interpret and give meaning to the narrative is a highly complex task (Goffman, 1959). Hence, the digital context can generate forms of 'suspended' narration, i.e., narration that needs an interpretative act on the part of the researcher and is therefore empirically controllable. The narration is also fragmented, since it is expressed in different forms and ways. Consequently, the researcher has the task of selecting, collecting, organizing, analysing and interpreting these new semantic units that underlie the micro-narrations of the Internet. Picking up from a difference proposed by Schütz (1967) between the agent subject who 'lives significantly in the social world' interpreting their own world and actions and 'the significant interpretation of such living through social sciences,' clearly, the categories of this dichotomy become more distant in the digital context. In light of these characteristics, it is not easy to interpret digital narratives, despite the fact that in recent years there has been a growing interest in the techniques recommended for analysing these types of narratives, as we will see in the following section.

5.4 Digital narratives and research methods

The increasingly valuable source of information, traces, data (Edwards et al., 2013; Rogers, 2013) provided by the development of digital technologies opens up new opportunities for investigating everyday life, social relationships, and identity, but at the same time gives rise to the need to reflect carefully on the traditional empirical apparatus of social enquiry. All these aspects, which encapsulate a variety of theoretical, methodological, technical, and ethical questions, converge in the analysis of the so-called 'digital sociology' that, according to Nortje Marres (2017), can take on three different and interrelated meanings.

The first concerns a substantive dimension: Digital sociology deals with the topics of social enquiry; it represents a fundamental societal phenomenon, since digitization affects every sphere of our life and determines societal, cultural, political, and economic changes. More specifically – as highlighted in the previous section – new digital technologies are embedded in multiple aspects of everyday life, creating new environments through which individuals can share the narratives of their life experience.

The second meaning relates to the platforms used for engaging with the audiences and public of sociology; in other words, digital sociology refers to the channels, contexts, and tools that sociologists use to communicate and share their knowledge with scientific communities and the public.

Finally, the last aspect of digital sociology – which is the specific subject of this section – focuses on the methods of social research, i.e., on the means and on the potential new ways of analysing contemporary society. The methodological challenges that underpin important epistemological issues are complex and delicate, given that they require the social researcher to tackle a complex mix of different elements, such as human beings, technological devices, infrastructure, and data. In this regard, using the idea expressed by Deborah Lupton,

> sociologists in general should develop new ways of 'doing sociology' in response to the digital age. If practitioners of the discipline are to retain their preeminent position as experts in social research, there are various ways of approaching research into the digital society. This is not to contend that more traditional social research methods should necessarily be discarded in favour of those using new digitized approaches. Sociologists should both investigate the various approaches that can be adopted to undertake digital social research and continue to question these approaches themselves for how they shape and interpret the data they produce (Lupton, 2014, pp. 42-43).

In order to move through the wide variety of research tools in the digital context, it is helpful to adopt the classification provided by Richard Rogers (2013) between the 'digitization' of methods and the 'natively digital' methods. The former refers to the many existing empirical research techniques that have been adapted for the web and the digital context: Web surveys, netnography, and network analysis represent, for example, the development of traditional techniques used in social research. This branch of methods also refers to the so-called digitized data objects, i.e., the information, traces, and data that have migrated to the web (Rogers, 2013). The second class of methods refers to the "natively digital" methods, which are the 'new' methods specifically designed according to the distinctive features of digital devices (Rogers, 2013). Within this discussion, Rogers also specifies that

> digital methods seek to learn from the so-called methods of the medium, that is, how online devices treat web data. Thus, digital methods are, first, the study of the methods embedded in the devices treating online data (Rogers, 2015, p. 2).

While the discussion on 'digitized methods' is quite entrenched, since it is based on assumptions and approaches that, although different, belong to the previous versions of traditional empirical research methods, the discussion on 'natively digital' methods is still open.

Regarding this aspect, Richard Rogers and his research group created the Digital Methods Initiative. They developed a set of tools designed to detect and analyse social network data and metadata, and to monitor online media outputs. Most of these are based on web 'scraping' in order to capture the digital traces. For example, the Twitter Capture and Analysis Toolset (DMI-TCAT) and Netvizz tools (Rieder, 2013) allow for the extraction of data from different sections of the social network platform for research purposes. Another interesting technique is that of issue mapping, aimed at the detection, analysis, and visualisation of contemporary current affairs on the Internet (Padovani, Pavan and Cernison, 2009; Rogers, 2013; Rogers, 2015).

Within this scenario, it is also necessary to underline that most of the techniques aimed at detecting and analysing the narrative dimension underlying the multiplicity and variety of data are based on quantitative methods, often of a textual nature. On this point, it is important to take into account the development of text mining approaches such as sentiment analysis, which is a computational analysis technique aimed at studying the "subjective elements in a language" (Ampofo et al., 2015, p. 166). In any case, computational automated research techniques run the risk of reducing the complex reality in which we exist, solely by mapping recurrence patterns, which sometimes do not provide significant results. For these reasons, according to the latest trends of social research, the complex dynamics of the online information produced could be explored by combining quantitative and qualitative methods into a broader methodology linking automated analysis with more adaptive methods (Ampofo et al., 2015).

One digital qualitative technique used to explore the discourses and the interactions on the Internet (often as a support of a quantitative technique) is netnography (Bowler, 2010; Kozinets, Dolbec and Earley, 2014; Bartl, Kannan and Stockinger, 2016). According to the classification of methods provided by Rogers, this is a digitalized method derived from traditional ethnography. According to Kozinets (2010, p. 7), netnography is in fact "a form of ethnographic research adapted to include the Internet's influence on contemporary social worlds." More specifically, it is participant-observational research based on online fieldwork that uses communications in the digital environment as a source of data to provide an ethnographic understanding and analysis of a cultural or communal phenomenon (Kozinets, 2010).

Netnography usually deals with the study of virtual communities; it allows the researcher, who is embedded in digital environments, to study social interactions online. The specific focus of this type of technique is the conversational acts of two or more people who express and share their opinions, culture, and feelings, developing specific visions of the world and a shared representation of identity. These conversations usually take place in forums, chats, and social networks that represent the field of this technique. Netnography has different, quite specific characteristics: For example, it usually enables the researcher to use a large and varied quantity of information that is easily available online; this also means that they could explore real-time conversations, which, since they are online, are constantly updated.

Compared to ethnography, netnography reduces the costs (e.g., travel expenses) and the time required for the entire search (gathering information, transcription of interviews). An important aspect of this type of technique is the non-intrusiveness of the researcher, who can observe and analyse the interactions between users in a non-invasive and sometimes anonymous way. Both the observation and analysis are delicate phases, due to the diversity and variety of information collected that can be in the form of texts, images, audio, and video. This highlights the highly complex nature of the empirical basis on which this technique is based. It therefore requires the researcher to be able to connect the multiplicity and variety of information and digital traces in a logical and coherent interpretative framework, identifying the narrative thread that ties them together. The need to gather many different elements is a typical feature of digital methods that call on researchers to organise and connect the semantic units that underpin these elements into a narrative plot.

While a large part of the discussion on digital methods focuses especially on techniques of collection and analysis, there seems to be less interest in the process of interpretation, which, in our opinion, plays a central role in attributing meaning to a heterogeneous set of data. In other words, it is necessary to use sociological imagination and heuristic procedures to try to identify the common thread through which to build a coherent and meaningful narrative structure.

The heuristic dimension required by the treatment of digital information could lead researchers to adopt an abductive method. Traditionally, social research has been based on either deductive or inductive reasoning. In the former, the hypotheses are deduced starting from a theoretical framework and are verified through empirical observation. In the second, broad generalizations are made from specific observations. Instead, abductive reasoning is a form of logical inference that starts from an observation and seeks to find the most likely explanation for it. In other words, it can be thought of as the "step of adopting a hypothesis as being suggested by the facts...a form of inference" (Peirce, 1998, p. 95). This type of reasoning produces new knowledge, i.e., information that is missing from the premises, and opens the way to new conclusions. Abduction also acts as inference or intuition and is directly aided and assisted by personal experience (Kolko, 2010). From this perspective, abduction can be traced back to a process based on clues that exploits and makes the best use of serendipity, understood as the ability of the eye to pick up a clue and to grasp an accidental idea, placing it within the framework of logical inferential reasoning (Sacchetti, 2012). In the same way, the manipulation, organization, analysis, and interpretation of digital traces can follow an abductive sensemaking reasoning based on observation and serendipity to come to the best explanation. The researcher hence identifies new semantic units in digital environments and in the heterogeneous, untidy, and unexpected multitude of traces and data, thus coming to an understanding of the relationships between the various elements and, more generally, among seemingly unrelated pieces of information.

In recent years, the landscape of digital narratives has undergone a significant transformation due to the growing influence of social media platforms and the emergence of large language models (LLMs) such as ChatGPT and similar AI-based tools. These technologies do not merely mediate social narratives – they actively generate, shape, and amplify them at unprecedented scale and speed (Gagrčin, 2024; Humphreys, 2018). From trending hashtags to algorithmically curated feeds, digital storytelling is increasingly co-produced by users, automated systems, and platform-specific logics.

This evolution raises important sociological questions about authorship, agency, and the construction of meaning. Narratives now emerge through a combination of user-generated content, algorithmic filtering, and platform conventions, creating new dynamics of visibility, fragmentation, and engagement (Abidin, 2021). Researchers must reconsider traditional narrative frameworks in light of these shifts, exploring how digital ecologies influence the way stories are told, circulated, and received.

The rise of LLMs adds a further layer of complexity. Tools like ChatGPT can assist students and researchers in generating text, summarizing content, experimenting with rhetorical styles, or simulating dialogic structures. However, their use also raises questions around originality, authorship, bias, and the epistemological status of machine-generated content. LLMs do not create narratives in a vacuum – they reflect training data shaped by historical, cultural, and ideological patterns, which must be made explicit in educational contexts.

Integrating these dimensions into the teaching of narrative methods can foster a more critical and reflexive approach to digital storytelling. Assignments that involve comparing human and AI-generated texts, analysing algorithmically mediated content, or tracing narrative diffusion across platforms can help students engage with the evolving nature of storytelling and understand the hybrid environments in which meaning is now produced and negotiated.

5.5 Navigating the intersection of sociology and narrative in the digital age

In this article, we have explored the relationship between sociology and narrativity. Narrative can reveal the voices of the individuals as they talk about their experiences and "construct identities (however multiple and changing) by locating themselves or being located within a repertoire of unplotted stories" (Somers, 1994, p. 614). In other words,

> people are guided to act in certain ways, and not others, on the basis of the projections, expectations, and memories derived from a multiplicity but ultimately limited repertoire of available social, public, and cultural narratives (Somers, 1994, p. 614).

We have also analysed how narrative takes on an even more significant connotation when contextualized in a contemporary society in which technologies are increasingly ubiquitous and are embedded in our everyday life. The contemporary individual indeed reflects and reshapes their own experiences through the narratives they often produce in digital contexts. This has led social researchers to use narrative practices to reduce the complexity of the world of shared and situated meanings.

From a methodological point of view, while traditional techniques are used to collect stories by "stimulating" them using the interview, the emergent digital techniques assume that digital technologies allow us to collect "directly" a set of traces, information, and data. The so-called data 'deluge' (Given, 2006; Savage and Burrows, 2007; Edwards et al., 2013) produced by the digitization of our lives poses several questions regarding the need to identify the narrative plot underlying such data.

Despite the quantity and variety of information, there is the perception that the new techniques of empirical research, while on the one hand enabling the reconstruction of general patterns of analysis, on the other hand return a fragmented narrative in which it is difficult to get back to the 'narrating self' and enter the depths of their vision of the world. It is therefore fundamental for the researcher to have the ability to connect the multiplicity of digital traces and contribute to the reflective interrogation of the empirical material emerging from digital contexts within a meaningful framework. Without a significant analytical and interpretative effort, the mass of information collected risks being reduced to a sterile aseptic synthesis of disconnected data. Therefore, it is necessary to rethink methods by linking them to the cognitive objectives that have always been central to sociologists, such as identity and everyday life (Lupton, 2014). Within this complex framework, sociologists, with their competence in social analysis, therefore, take on a central role in the design and implementation of suitable tools to detect, analyse, and interpret the complexity of digital societies at situated, networked, and system levels (Housley et al., 2017), connecting methodological issues to ontological, epistemological, and ethical issues.

Conclusion

While traditional methods are still relevant, they are increasingly complemented by innovative techniques that utilize digital technology. The fourth chapter demonstrates the transformative potential of digital narratives in empirical research. This chapter not only provides a theoretical framework but also discusses practical applications and shows how digital narratives can enrich our understanding of social phenomena.

To summarize, the future of qualitative research lies in the integration of traditional and digital methods. Sociologists must continue to adapt and innovate so that their research methods remain relevant and robust in an ever-evolving digital society. The discussions in this book aim to equip researchers with the knowledge and tools they need to navigate this complex landscape and promote a deeper and more nuanced understanding of the social world.

Data visualisation is essential in modern social research to explore, communicate, and interpret complex social phenomena. Future efforts should focus on personalizing learning, integrating theory and practice, providing continuous feedback and strengthening data visualisation courses at the beginning of academic training. Effective teaching in data visualisation prepares students to maximize their potential in research and social practice.

The use of technology in higher education has greatly increased with the development of various forms of online education, such as e-learning and distance education. Numerous studies and experiences show that it is not enough to simply transfer traditional teaching into a digital format (Ehlers and Pawlowski, 2006; Kirkwood and Price, 2014; Lupton, Mewburn and Thomson, 2017). This process involves a variety of actors, decisions, factors, and dimensions at both the micro and macro levels.

During the completion of this editorial project, the COVID-19 pandemic changed lives around the world (Diana, Ferrari and Dommarco, 2021). The mass closure of universities led to rapid crisis response measures to ensure the continuity of courses, resulting in a rapid transition to online teaching and learning. These emergency measures differed significantly from the time and effort normally required to deliver a high-quality course. As a result, the socio-educational component was often marginalized in favour of technical solutions to deal with the immediate crisis.

Teachers had to rethink their teaching methods, not only in terms of content and tools, but also in terms of their relationship with students and their role as educators during the emergency. This situation raised critical issues: the need for digital skills, the decontextualization of knowledge through datafication processes (Williamson, Bayne and Shay, 2020), building relationships with students in a 'disembodied' environment and the construction of intellectual growth pathways in an 'on-demand' education system.

Looking to the future, the development of e-learning courses for distance education must involve collaborative planning between different stakeholders, ensuring that theoretical, epistemological and methodological perspectives are not ignored (Diana and Ferrari, 2023). This book has highlighted the key elements that characterize the teaching of social research methodology in sociology courses. It has considered the changes in the field, the profile of students, and their evaluation of the usefulness of the course in terms of the skills acquired.

In developing our studies on the teaching of social research methodology, it is crucial to offer our assessments to a specialized audience, especially in times of crisis, to prevent the discipline's knowledge and learning models from being challenged by technological and algorithmic solutions used by e-learning platforms.

Finally, I would like to reflect on the scenarios that Artificial Intelligence (AI) could create in the teaching of social research methodology and in education in general. The application of AI to the organization, analysis, and visualisation of data opens new perspectives and possibilities for social research methodology. AI-driven tools can improve research by providing sophisticated means to process vast amounts of data and uncover patterns that are not visible using traditional methods. However, these advances also bring critical challenges. The lure of methodological shortcuts offered by AI can lead to a loss of reflexivity and interpretative depth (De Luca Picione et al., 2023). While AI can automate many aspects of data processing, maintaining a critical approach is essential to preserve data quality and interpretive richness. Researchers must ensure that the convenience of AI tools does not overshadow the need for thorough and thoughtful analysis.

In conclusion, the integration of traditional and digital methods represents the future of social research. This book aims to inspire and empower researchers to adapt and navigate this evolving landscape to ensure that social research remains relevant, robust and responsive to the complexities of the digital age. The journey of adaptation and innovation in social research methods is not over, and this volume serves as a comprehensive resource for those seeking to advance the field.

Bibliography

Abbott, A., 2004. *Methods of discovery: Heuristics for the social sciences*. W.W. Norton and Company.

Abidin, C., 2021. Mapping Internet Celebrity on TikTok: Exploring Attention Economies and Visibility Labours. *Cultural Science Journal, 12*(1): 77-103. https://doi.org/10.5334/csci.140

Addeo, F. and Diana, P., 2010. La méthode des « Histoires »: une approche mixte de la collecte et de l'analyse de données sur les valeurs. *Cahiers de praxématique*, 54-55: 263-282. https://doi.org/10.4000/praxematique.1174

Addeo, F. and Montesperelli, P., 2007. *Esperienze di analisi di interviste non direttive*. Aracne.

Adriaensen, J., Kerremans, B. and Slootmaeckers, K., 2015. Editors' introduction to the thematic issue: Mad about methods? Teaching research methods in political science. *Journal of Political Science Education, 11*(1):1-10. https://doi.org/10.1080/15512169.2014.985017

Aguado, N.A., 2009. Teaching research methods: Learning by doing. *Journal of Public Affairs Education, 15*(2): 251-260. https://doi.org/10.1080/15236803.2009.12001557

Alvarez, I., Guasch, T. and Espasa, A., 2009. University teacher roles and competencies in online learning environments: a theoretical analysis of teaching and learning practices. *European Journal of Teacher Education, 32*(3): 321-336. https://doi.org/10.1080/02619760802624104

Al Zumor, A. W. Q., Al Refaai, I. K., Eddin, E. A. B. and Al-Rahman, F. H. A., 2013. EFL students' perceptions of a blended learning environment: Advantages, limitations and suggestions for improvement. *English Language Teaching, 6*(10): 95-110. https://doi.org/10.5539/elt.v6n10p95

Ala-Mutka, K., 2011. *Mapping digital competence: Towards a conceptual understanding*. Luxembourg: Publications Office of the European Union. http://www.jrc.ec.europa.eu [Accessed 7 June 2024].

Amaturo, E. and Aragona, B., 2019. Per un'epistemologia del digitale: Note sull'uso di big data e computazione nella ricerca sociale. *Quaderni di Sociologia, 81*(LXIII): 71-90. https://doi.org/10.4000/qds.3508

Amendola, S., Errichiello, N., and Vitale, M. P., 2005. E-Learning: l'esperienza della Facoltà di Lettere dell'Università di Salerno. In atti di *Expo 2005, E-learning: protagonista dello sviluppo della società della conoscenza* (pp. 1-8). Tecomproject Editore Multimediale – Omniacom.

Ammenwerth, E., 2017. Envisioning changing role of university teacher in online instructional environments. *AISHE-J: The All Ireland Journal of Teaching and Learning in Higher Education, 9*(3): 3121-3129.

Ampofo, L., Collister, S., O'Loughlin, B. and Chadwick, A., 2015. Text Mining and Social Media: When Quantitative Meets Qualitative, and Software Meets People. In P. Halfpenny, and R. Procter (Eds.), *Innovations in Digital Research Methods* (pp. 161-192). Sage. https://doi.org/10.4135/9781473920651.n8

Anderson, J., 2005. IT, e-learning and teacher development. *International Education Journal*, 5(5): 1-14.

Arcangeli, B., and Diana, P., 2008. Cultural capital, learning and ICT in a southern Italian university. In M. C. Matteucci, A. Omicini, E. Nardini, and P. Gaffuri (Eds.), *Proceedings: Knowledge Construction in E-learning Context: CSCL, ODL, ICT and SNA in education 2008* (pp. 176-180). RWTH Aachen University.

Arcangeli, B. and Diana, P., 2009. Insegnare metodologia delle scienze sociali in modalità e-learning. In: A. Baldissera, (Ed.). *Insegnare metodologia delle Scienze Sociali*. Bonanno. pp. 55-71.

Arvanitis, E., 2018. Preservice teacher education: Towards a transformative and reflexive learning. *Global Studies of Childhood*, 8(2): 114-130. https://doi.org/10.1177/2043610617734980

Atkinson, M. P. and Hunt, A. N., 2008. Inquiry-guided learning in sociology. *Teaching Sociology*, 36(1): 1-7. https://doi.org/10.1177/0092055X0803600101

Atkinson, R., 1998. *The life story interview*. Sage Publications. https://doi.org/10.4135/9781412986205

Auster, C. J., 2016. Blended learning as a potentially winning combination of face-to-face and online learning: An exploratory study. *Teaching Sociology*, 44(1): 39-48. https://doi.org/10.1177/0092055X15619217

Bailyn, L., 1977. Research as a cognitive process: Implications for data analysis. *Quality and Quantity*, 11(2): 97-117. https://doi.org/10.1007/BF00151906

Barbera, F., 2006. L'immaginazione sociologica rivisitata: Le euristiche per la scoperta nelle scienze sociali. *Quaderni di Sociologia*, 41: 165-174. https://doi.org/10.4000/qds.1038

Barraket, J., 2005. Teaching research method using a student-centred approach? Critical reflections on practice. *Journal of University Teaching and Learning Practice*, 2(2): 64-74. https://doi.org/10.53761/1.2.2.3

Bartl, M., Kannan, V. K., and Stockinger, H., 2016. A review and analysis of literature on netnography research. *International Journal of Technology Marketing*, 11(2): 165-196. https://doi.org/10.1504/IJTMKT.2016.075687

Bastian, M., Heymann, S., and Jacomy, M. 2009. Gephi: an open-source software for exploring and manipulating networks. In *Proceedings of the international AAAI conference on web and social media*, 3(1): 361-362. https://doi.org/10.1609/icwsm.v3i1.13937

Bauman, Z., 2006. *Liquid times: Living in an age of uncertainty*. Polity Press.

Bechhofer, F., 1974. Current approaches to empirical research: Some central ideas. In: J. Rex, (Ed.), *Approaches to sociology: An introduction to major trends in British sociology*, (pp. 70-91). Routledge.

Beck, U., 1992. *Risk society: Towards a new modernity*. Sage.

Beetham, H. and Sharpe, R., (Eds.), 2007. *Rethinking pedagogy for a digital age: Designing and delivering e-learning*. Routledge. https://doi.org/10.4324/9780203961681

Bennato, D., 2012. *Sociologia dei media digitali: relazioni sociali e processi comunicativi del web partecipativo*. Editori Laterza.

Bennato, D., 2015. *Il computer come macroscopio. Big data e approccio computazionale per comprendere i cambiamenti sociali e culturali*. FrancoAngeli.

Bertaux, D., 1981. *Biography and society: The life history approach in the social sciences*. Sage Publications.

Besozzi, E. and Colombo, M., 2014. *Metodologia della ricerca sociale nei contesti socio-educativi*. Guerini and Associati.

Bichi, R., 2000. *La società raccontata: metodi biografici e vite complesse*. Franco Angeli.

Bichi, R., 2005. *La conduzione delle interviste nella ricerca sociale*. Carocci.

Bingham, W. V., and Moore, B. V., 1931. *How to interview*. Harper & Brothers.

Bingimlas, K. A., 2009. Barriers to the successful integration of ICT in teaching and learning environments: A review of the literature. *Eurasia Journal of Mathematics, science and technology education*, 5(3): 235-245. https://doi.org/10.12973/ejmste/75275

Bobek, E. and Tversky, B., 2016. Creating visual explanations improves learning. *Cognitive Research: Principles and Implications*, 1(27): 1-14. https://doi.org/10.1186/s41235-016-0031-6

Boccia Artieri, G., 2012. *Stati di connessione. Pubblici, cittadini e consumatori nella (Social) Network Society*. FrancoAngeli.

Boccia Artieri, G., Gemini, L., Pasquali, F., Carlo, S., Farci, M. and Pedroni, M., 2018. *Fenomenologia dei social network. Presenza, relazioni e consumi mediali degli italiani online*. Guerini and Associati.

Bonaiuti, G. (Ed.), 2006. *E-learning 2.0: il futuro dell'apprendimento in rete fra formale e informale*. Edizioni Erickson.

Bonet, E., 2005. Book Review: B. Czarniawska, Narratives in Social Science Research. *Management Learning*, 36(4): 523-531. https://doi.org/10.1177/135050760503600409

Bowler, G. M., 2010. Netnography: A method specifically designed to study cultures and communities online. *The Qualitative Report*, 15(5): 1270-1275.

Braguglia, K. II. and Jackson, K. A., 2012. Teaching research methodology using a project-based three-course sequence: Critical reflections on practice. *American Journal of Business Education*, 5(3): 347-352. https://doi.org/10.19030/ajbe.v5i3.7007

Briggs, L. T., Brown, S. E., Gardner, R. B. and Davidson, R. L., 2009. D.RA.MA: An extended conceptualization of student anxiety in criminal justice research methods courses. *Journal of Criminal Justice Education*, 20(3): 217-226. https://doi.org/10.1080/10511250903109348

Broers, N.J., 2002. Selection and use of propositional knowledge in statistical problem-solving. *Learning and Instruction*, 12: 323-344. https://doi.org/10.1016/S0959-4752(01)00025-1

Broman, K. W. and Woo, K. H., 2018. Data organization in spreadsheets. *The American Statistician*, 72(1): 2-10. https://doi.org/10.1080/00031305.2017.1375989

Brown, M. E., 1979. Sociology as critical theory. In: S.G. McNall, (Ed.), *Theoretical perspectives in sociology* (pp. 251-275). St. Martin's.

Bruner, J. S., 1986. *Actual minds, possible worlds*. Harvard University Press. https://doi.org/10.4159/9780674029019

Bruschi, B., and Ercole, M. L., 2005. *Strategie per l'e-learning. Progettare e valutare la formazione on-line*. Carocci.

Bruschi, B. and Ranieri, M., 2018. University education: quality, effectiveness, teacher training. *Form@ re-Open Journal per la formazione in rete, 18*(1): 1-6.

Buffardi, A., and De Kerckhove, D., 2011. *Il sapere digitale: pensiero ipertestuale e conoscenza connettiva*. Liguori.

Bulmer, M. and Burgess, R. G., 1981. Which way forward for methodology teaching?. *Sociology, 15*(4): 586-589. https://doi.org/10.1177/0038038581015 00416

Burgess, R. G., 1981. Objectives in teaching and using research methodology. *Sociology, 15*(4): 490-495. https://doi.org/10.1177/003803858101500402

Burgess, R. G., 1990. Sociologists, training and research. *Sociology*, 24: 579-595. https://doi.org/10.1177/0038038590024004002

Burgess, R. G. and Bulmer, M., 1981. Research methodology teaching: Trends and developments. *Sociology*, 15: 477-489. https://doi.org/10.1177/00380385 8101500401

Caliandro, A. and Gandini, A., 2019. *I metodi digitali nella ricerca sociale*. Carocci.

Calvani, A., 2010. *Innovazione tecnologica e cambiamento dell'università*. University Press.

Calvani, A., and Rotta, M., 2003. *Fare formazione in Internet: manuale di didattica online*. Edizioni Erickson.

Capogna, S., 2014. *Scuola, Università, E-learning: un'analisi sociologica*. Armando.

Capogna, S., 2016. Schools 2.0: Experiences and Expertise. Digital Teachers Wanted. *Italian Journal of Sociology of Education, 8*(2): 54-67. https://doi.org/10.146 58/pupj-ijse-2016-2-4

Capogna, S., 2017. Communication for education. From teacher to facilitator in learning and discovery processes. *JANUS. NET, e-journal of International Relations, 8*(2): 123-128. https://doi.org/10.26619/1647-7251.8.2.01

Catelani, M., Formiconi, A. R., Ranieri, M., Pezzati, F., Raffaghelli, J. E., and Bruni, I., 2018. Promuovere l'innovazione didattica e lo sviluppo professionale della docenza universitaria: primi risultati dello sportello e-learning dell'Università di Firenze. In A. Volungeviciene and A. Szűcs (Eds.), *Exploring the Micro, Meso and Macro Proceedings of the European Distance and E-Learning Network 2018, Annual Conference Genova* (pp. 761-770).

Catone, M. C., and Diana, P., 2016. L'esperienza del corso blended di metodologia delle scienze sociali: la voce degli student. In M. Rui, L. Messina and T. Minerva (Eds.), *Teach different! Proceedings della Multiconferenza EMEMITALIA 2015* (pp. 379-382). Genova University Press.

Catone, M. C. and Diana, P., 2017. Social Research Methods 2.0: e-learning design. *Journal of e-Learning and Knowledge Society, 13*(3): 9-22. https://doi. org/10.20368/1971-8829/1380

Catone, M. C. and Diana, P., 2019a. I domini della competenza digitale tra numeracy e analisi sociale nella formazione universitaria. In L. De Nicolai and A. Parola, (Eds.), *Digital Education: ricerca, pratiche ed esperienza nei mondi mediali* (pp. 73-80). Aracne.

Catone, M. C. and Diana, P., 2019b. Narrative in social research: Between tradition and innovation. *Italian Journal of Sociology of Education, 11*(2): 14-33.

Catone, M. C. and Diana, P., 2019c. Expansion and reconfiguration of the action of the university teacher in relation to ICT: A qualitative analysis. *Italian Journal of Sociology of Education*, *11*(1): 20-45.

Catone, M. C. and Diana, P., 2020. *Teaching social research methods in digital contexts*. L'Harmattan.

Cazzanti, R., 2016. *Open data e nativi digitali: per un uso intelligente delle tecnologie*. libreriauniversitaria.it Edizioni.

Chao, I. T., Saj, T. and Hamilton, D., 2010. Using collaborative course development to achieve online course quality standards, *The International Review of Research in Open and Distributed Learning*, *11*(3): 106-126. https://doi.org/10.19173/irrodl.v11i3.912

Clandinin, D. J. and Connelly, F. M., 2000. *Narrative inquiry. Experience and story in qualitative research*. Jossey-bass.

Collins, R., 1992. *Sociological insight: An introduction to non-obvious sociology*. Oxford University Press.

Colombo, M., (Ed.), 2008. *E-learning e cambiamenti sociali: dal competere al comprendere*. Liguori.

Connelly, F. M., and Clandinin, D. J., 2007. Teacher education: A question of teacher knowledge. Tomorrow's teachers: International and critical perspectives on teacher education. In J. Freeman-Moir, and A. Scott, *Shaping the future: Critical essays on teacher education* (pp. 89-105). Brill. https://doi.org/10.11 63/9789087903565_008

Corazza, L., 2006. E-learning e Università. Riflessioni tratte dalle interviste a quattro esperti italiani: Antonio Calvani, Luigi Guerra, Roberto Maragliano, Pier Cesare Rivoltella. *Ricerche di Pedagogia e Didattica*, 1: 111-125. https:// doi/org/10.1400/172537

Corbetta, P., 2003. *Social research: Theory, methods and techniques*. Sage. https://doi.org/10.4135/9781849209922

Creswell, J. W. and Plano Clark, V. L., 2023. Revisiting mixed methods research designs twenty years later. In Poth, C. N., *Handbook of mixed methods research designs* (pp. 21-36). Sage. https://doi.org/10.4135/9781529614572.n6

Crooks, V. A., Castleden, H. and Meerveld, I. T. V., 2010. Teaching research methods courses in human geography: Critical reflections. *Journal of Geography in Higher Education*, *34*(2): 155-171. https://doi.org/10.1080/0309826090309 3646

Crotti, M., 2017. La riflessività nella formazione alla professione docente. *Edetania. Estudios y propuestas socioeducativas*, 52: 85-106.

Czarniawska, B., 2004. *Narratives in social science research*. Sage Publications. https://doi.org/10.4135/9781849209502

Cutler, S. J., 1987. The A.C.E. freshman survey as a baseline instrument for survey projects in research methods courses. *Teaching Sociology*, 15: 121-127. https://doi.org/10.2307/1318025

Dabbagh, N., 2005. Pedagogical models for e-learning: A theory-based design framework. International *Journal of Technology in Teaching and Learning*, *1*(1): 25-44.

Dabbagh, N. and Bannan-Ritland, B., 2005. *Online learning: Concepts, strategies, and application*. Upper Saddle River, NJ: Pearson/Merrill/Prentice Hall.

Daniel, B. K., 2018a. Contestable professional academic identity of those who teach research methodology. *International Journal of Research and Method in Education*, *41*(5): 548-561. https://doi.org/10.1080/1743727X.2017.1369510

Daniel, B. K., 2018b. Reimaging research methodology as data science. *Big Data and Cognitive Computing*, *2*(1). https://doi.org/10.3390/bdcc2010004

Daniel, B., Kumar, V. and Omar, N., 2018. Postgraduate conception of research methodology: Implications for learning and teaching. *International Journal of Research and Method in Education*, *41*(2): 220-236. https://doi.org/10.10 80/1743727X.2017.1283397

De Luca Picione, G. L., Diana, P., Ferrari, G., Fortini, L. and Trezza, D., 2023. IA Generativa nel welfare: un approccio basato sulla Sociologia Pubblica per una governance consapevole, *Cambio. Rivista sulle Trasformazioni Sociali*, *13*(26). https://oaj.fupress.net/index.php/cambio/article/view/15358 [Accessed 7 June 2024].

Diana, P. and Catone, M. C., 2016. E-learning in an undergraduate course in research methods for the social sciences: Reflections on teaching. *Italian Journal of Sociology of Education*, *8*(2): 110-142. https://doi.org/10.36253/cambio-15358

Diana, P. and Catone, M. C., 2018. Innovations in teaching social research methods at the university in the digital era: An Italian case study. *Italian Journal of Sociology of Education*, *10*(1): 128-165.

Diana, P. and Ferrari, G., 2023. Il dibattito sulla ricerca sociale pubblica in Italia. Storia, Profili, Prospettive. *Cambio. Rivista Sulle Trasformazioni Sociali*, *13*(26). https://oaj.fupress.net/index.php/cambio/issue/view/894 [Accessed 7 June 2024]. https://doi.org/10.36253/cambio-16234

Diana, P. and Ferrari, G., 2024. La ricerca sociale pubblica in Italia attraverso i percorsi di istituzionalizzazione: una ricostruzione introduttiva. *Cambio. Rivista Sulle Trasformazioni Sociali*, *13*(26). https://oaj.fupress.net/index. php/cambio/article/view/16234 [Accessed 7 June 2024]. https://doi.org/10. 36253/cambio-16234

Diana, P., Ferrari, G., and Dommarco, P., 2021. *COVID-19. Un mutamento sociale epocale*. Novalogos.

Diana, P., and Montesperelli, P., 2005. *Analizzare le interviste ermeneutiche*. Carocci.

Earley, M. A., 2014. A synthesis of the literature on research methods education. *Teaching in Higher Education*, *19*(3): 242-253. https://doi.org/10.1080/13562 517.2013.860105

Edelmann, A., Wolff, T., Montagne, D., and Bail, C. A., 2020. Computational social science and sociology. *Annual review of sociology*, *46*(1): 61-81. https://doi.org/10.1146/annurev-soc-121919-054621

Edwards, A., Housley, W., Williams, M., Sloan, L. and Williams, M., 2013. Digital social research, social media and the sociological imagination: surrogacy, augmentation and re-orientation. *International Journal of Social Research Methodology*, *16*(3): 245-260. https://doi.org/10.1080/13645579.2013.774185

Ehlers, U. D., 2013. *Open learning cultures: A guide to quality, evaluation, and assessment for future learning*. Springer. https://doi.org/10.1007/978-3-642-38174-4

Ehlers, U. D. and Pawlowski, J. M., (Eds.), 2006. *Handbook on quality and standardization in e-learning*. Springer. https://doi.org/10.1007/3-540-32788-6

Ehlers, U. D., 2004. Quality in E-Learning. The Learners Perspective. *European Journal of Open, Distance and E-Learning (EURODL)*, 1: 1-7.

El-Najjar, H.A., 2018. Online teaching in sociology: Prospects, successes, and problems. *The Journal of Public and Professional Sociology*, *10*(1): 3. https://doi.org/10.62915/2154-8935.1126

Elliott, J., 2005. *Using narrative in social research: Qualitative and quantitative approaches*. Sage Publications.

Engebretsen, M., and Kennedy, H., 2020. *Data visualisation in society*. Amsterdam University Press. https://doi.org/10.1515/9789048543137

European Commission, 2022. *The Digital Services Act (DSA) – Regulation (EU) 2022/2065*. European Commission.

European Parliament and Council of the European Union, 2016. *Regulation (EU) 2016/679: General Data Protection Regulation (GDPR)*, L119.

European Parliament and the Council, 2006. Recommendation of the European Parliament and of the Council of 18 December 2006 on key competences for lifelong learning. *Official Journal of the European Union*, 394/310.

Fabbri, L., 2007. *Comunità di pratiche e apprendimento riflessivo. Per una formazione situata*. Carocci.

Farkas, M., 2012. Participatory technologies, pedagogy 2.0 and information literacy. *Library Hi Tech*, 30: 82-94. https://doi.org/10.1108/07378831211213229

Felisatti, E. and Serbati, A., 2014. Professionalità docente e innovazione didattica. Una proposta dell'Università di Padova per lo sviluppo professionale dei docenti universitari. Formazione and Insegnamento. *Rivista internazionale di Scienze dell'educazione e della formazione*, *12*(1): 137-153.

Ferreira, C. M. and Serpa, S., 2017. Challenges in the teaching of sociology in higher education: Contributions to a discussion. *Societies*, *7*(4), 30: 1-11. https://doi.org/10.3390/soc7040030

Ferri, P., 2001. *Nativi digitali*. Bruno Mondadori.

Fideli, R. and Marradi, A., 1996. Intervista, in AA. VV., *Enciclopedia delle Scienze Sociali*, vol. 5. Istituto dell'Enciclopedia Italiana.

Floridi, L., Cowls, J., Beltrametti, et al., 2018. AI4People – An ethical framework for a good AI society: Opportunities, risks, principles, and recommendations. *Minds and Machines*, *28*(1): 689-707. https://doi.org/10.1007/s11023-018-9482-5

Fontes, L.A. and Piercy, F.P., 2000. Engaging students in qualitative research through experiential class activities. *Teaching of Psychology*, *27*(3): 174-179. https://doi.org/10.1207/S15328023TOP2703_03

Friendly, M. and Wainer, H., 2021. *A history of data visualisation and graphic communication*. Harvard University Press. https://doi.org/10.4159/97806742 59034

Gaebel, M., Kupriyanova, V., Morais, R., and Colucci, E., 2014. *E-Learning in European Higher Education Institutions: Results of a Mapping Survey Conducted in October-December 2013*. European University Association.

Gagrčin, E., 2024. Your social ties, your personal public sphere, your responsibility: How users construe a sense of personal responsibility for intervention against uncivil comments on Facebook. *New Media & Society, 26*(8): 4299-4316. https://doi.org/10.1177/14614448221117499

Gal, I., Alatorre, S., Close, S., Evans, J., Johansen, L., Maguire, T., Manly, M., and Tout, D., 2009. PIAAC Numeracy: A Conceptual Framework. *OECD Education Working Papers*, 35. OECD Publishing (NJ1).

Galliani L., 2011. Progettare e gestire nuove forme di didattica in un'Università cambiata. In L. Galliani (Ed.), *Il Docente Universitario. Una professione tra ricerca, didattica e governance degli Atenei* (pp. 145-158). Pensa MultiMedia.

Gardner, H., and Davis, K., 2014. *Generazione app. La testa dei giovani e il nuovo mondo digitale.* Milano.

Garrison, D.R., and Kanuka, H., 2004. Blended learning: Uncovering its transformative potential in higher education. *The internet and higher education, 7*(2): 95-105. https://doi.org/10.1016/j.iheduc.2004.02.001

Geer, R., 2009. Strategies for blended approaches in teacher education. In *Effective blended learning practices: evidence-based perspectives in ICT-facilitated education* (pp. 39-61). IGI Global. https://doi.org/10.4018/978-1-60566-296-1.ch003

Giddens, A., 1991. *Modernity and self-identity: Self and society in the late modern age.* Stanford University Press.

Ghislandi, P.M., Raffaghelli, J, and Cumer, F., 2012. La qualità dell'eLearning. Un approccio qualitativo per l'analisi dei feedback degli studenti e dei docenti. *Ricerche di Pedagogia e Didattica, 7*(2): 25-47.

Ghislandi, P. and Raffaghelli, J., 2013. La voce degli studenti per la qualità dell'e-learning nella formazione universitaria: Un approccio partecipativo. In: V., Grion and A., Cook-Sather, (Eds.), *Student voice: Prospettive internazionali e pratiche emergenti in Italia* (pp. 273-286). Guerini Scientifica.

Gillis, A. and Krull, L.M., 2020. COVID-19 remote learning transition in spring 2020: Class structures, student perceptions, and inequality in college courses. *Teaching Sociology*, pp. 1-17. https://doi.org/10.1177/0092055X20954263

Giordano, G., and Vitale, M., 2006. Multidimensional Data Analysis to assess interactions in an e-learning community. *Journal of e-learning and knowledge society, 2*(2): 191-204.

Given, J., 2006. Narrating the Digital Turn: data deluge, technomethodology, and other likely tales. *Qualitative Sociology Review, 2*(1): 54-65. https://doi.org/10.18778/1733-8077.2.1.05

Gobo, G., 2009. La didattica multimediale: Ipotesi, esperienze, suggerimenti. In: A. Baldissera, (Ed.) *Insegnare metodologia delle Scienze Sociali* (pp. 87-102). Bonanno.

Goffman, E., 1959. *The presentation of self in everyday life.* Anchor Books.

Gogan, M. L., Sirbu, R. and Draghici, A., 2015. Aspects concerning the use of the Moodle platform: Case study. *Procedia Technology*, 19: 1142-1148. https://doi.org/10.1016/j.protcy.2015.02.163

Gray, D. E., 2021. *Doing Research in the Real World.* SAGE Publications.

Grion, V., 2016. Conclusion: higher education, participation and change. In M. Fedeli, V. Grion, and D. Frison (Eds.), *Coinvolgere per apprendere Metodi e tecniche partecipative per la formazione* (pp. 359-370). PensaMultimedia.

Guidicini, P., 1968. *Manuale della ricerca sociologica.* Franco Angeli.

Halford, S. and Savage, M., 2017. Speaking sociologically with big data: Symphonic social science and the future for big data research. *Sociology*, *51*(6): 1132-1148. https://doi.org/10.1177/0038038517698639

Halfpenny, P., 1981. Teaching ethnographic data analysis on postgraduate courses in sociology. *Sociology*, *15*(4): 564-570. https://doi.org/10.1177/00380385810 1500413

Halasz, J.R. and Kaufman, P., 2008. Sociology as pedagogy: How ideas from the discipline can inform teaching and learning. *Teaching Sociology*, *36*(4): 301-317. https://doi.org/10.1177/0092055X0803600401

Hammersley, M., 2012. Is it possible to teach social research methods well today. *Social Sciences Teaching and Learning Summit: Teaching Research Methods*, University of Warwick, 21-22 June 2012. https://martynhammersley. files.wordpress.com/2013/03/hammersley-hea-paper-teaching-research-methods.pdf [Accessed 7 June 2024].

Hanson, C., 2005. The scholarship of teaching and learning done by sociologists: Let's make that the sociology of higher education. *Teaching Sociology*, *33*(4): 411-416. https://doi.org/10.1177/0092055X0503300408

Harasim, L., 2012. *Learning theory and online technologies*. Routledge. https:// doi.org/10.4324/9780203846933

Harjanto, A.S. and Sumarni, S., 2019. Teachers' experiences on the use of Google Classroom. *English Language and Literature International Conference (ELLiC) Proceedings*, 3: 172-178.

Harley, K. and Natalier, K., 2013. Teaching sociology: Reflections on the discipline. *Journal of Sociology*, *49*(4): 389-396. https://doi.org/10.1177/1440783313504049

Healy, K. and Moody, J., 2014. Data visualisation in sociology. *Annual Review of Sociology*, 40: 105-128. https://doi.org/10.1146/annurev-soc-071312-145551

Hénard, F., and Roseveare, D., 2012. Fostering quality teaching in higher education: Policies and Practices. An *IMHE Guide for Higher Education Institutions*. Oecd.

Holt, D., and Segrave, S., 2003. Creating and sustaining quality e-learning environments of enduring value for teachers and learners. In G., Crisp, D., Thiele, I., Scholten, S., Barker and J., Baron (Eds.), *Interact, Integrate, Impact: Proceedings of the 20th Annual Conference of the Australasian Society for Computers in Learning in Tertiary Education*. Adelaide, 7-10 December 2003 (pp. 226-235). Ascilite.

Housley, W., Dicks, B., Henwood, K. and Smith, R., 2017. Qualitative methods and data in digital societies. *Qualitative Research*, *17*(6): 607-609. https://doi. org/10.1177/1468794117730936

Humphreys, L., 2018. *The Qualified Self: Social Media and the Accounting of Everyday Life*. MIT Press. https://doi.org/10.7551/mitpress/9780262037853. 001.0001

Hyvärinen, M., 2016. Narrative and sociology. *Narrative Works*, *6*(1): 38-62.

Jedlowski, P., 2000. *Storie comuni. La narrazione della vita quotidiana*. Milano.

Jarke, J. and Breiter, A., 2019. *The datafication of education. Learning, Media and Technology*, *44*(1): 1-6. https://doi.org/10.1080/17439884.2019.1573833

Jonassen, D.H., 1994. Thinking technology: Toward a constructivist design model. *Educational Technology*, *34*(3): 34-37.

Keenan, K. and Fontaine, D., 2012. Listening to our students: Understanding how they learn research methods in geography. *Journal of Geography, 111*(6): 224-235. https://doi.org/10.1080/00221341.2011.653651

Kilburn, D., Nind, M. and Wiles, R., 2014. Learning as researchers and teachers: The development of a pedagogical culture for social science research methods? *British Journal of Educational Studies, 62*(2): 191-207. https://doi.org/10.10 80/00071005.2014.918576

King, A., 2015. Some notes about teaching Sociology online. *Социология науки и технологий, 6*(2): 92-96.

Kirkwood, A., 2009. E-learning: You don't always get what you hope for. *Technology, Pedagogy and Education, 18*(2): 107-121. https://doi.org/10.1080/147593909 02992576

Kirkwood, A. and Price, L., 2014. Technology-enhanced learning and teaching in higher education: What is 'enhanced' and how do we know? A critical literature review. *Learning, Media and Technology, 39*(1): 6-36. https://doi. org/10.1080/17439884.2013.770404

Kitchin, R., 2014. Big data, new epistemologies and paradigm shifts. *Big Data and Society, 1*(1): 1-12. https://doi.org/10.1177/2053951714528481

Kolko, J., 2010. Abductive thinking and sensemaking: The drivers of design synthesis. *Design issues, 26*(1): 15-28. https://doi.org/10.1162/desi.2010.26.1.15

Koehler, M. J. and Mishra, P., 2005. What happens when teachers design educational technology? The development of technological pedagogical content knowledge. *Journal of Educational Computing Research, 32*(2): 131-152. https://doi.org/10.2190/0EW7-01WB-BKHL-QDYV

Koehler, M.J. and Mishra, P., 2008. Introducing TPCK. In: *AACTE Committee on Innovation and Technology, ed. The handbook of technological pedagogical content knowledge (TPCK) for educators* (pp. 3-29). American Association of Colleges of Teacher Education and Routledge.

Kozinets, R. V., 1998. On netnography: Initial reflections on consumer research investigations of cyberculture. *Advances in consumer research, 25*(1): 366-371.

Kozinets, R. V., 2010. *Netnography: Doing ethnographic research online.* Sage Publications.

Kozinets, R. V., Dolbec, P. Y. and Earley, A., 2014. Netnographic analysis: Understanding culture through social media data. In U. Flick, (Ed.), *The SAGE handbook of qualitative data analysis,* (pp. 262-276). Sage Publications. https://doi.org/10.4135/9781446282243.n18

Latour, B., Jensen, P., Venturini, T., Grauwin, S. and Boullier, D., 2012. 'The whole is always smaller than its parts': A digital test of Gabriel Tarde's monads. *The British Journal of Sociology, 63*(4): 590-615. https://doi.org/10.1111/j.1468-4446.2012.01428.x

Laurillard, D., 2012. *Teaching as a design science. building pedagogical patterns for learning and technology.* Routledge, Taylor and Francis Group.

Laurillard, D., 1995. Multimedia and the changing experience of the learner. *British Journal of Educational Technology, 26*(3): 179-189. https://doi.org/10. 1111/j.1467-8535.1995.tb00340.x

Lave, J. and Wenger, E., 2006. *L'apprendimento situato: Dall'osservazione alla partecipazione attiva nei contesti sociali.* Edizioni Erickson.

Lazer, D., Pentland, A., Adamic, L., Aral, S., Barabási, A. L., Brewer, D. et al., 2009. Computational social science. *Science, 323*(5915): 721-723. https://doi.org/10.1126/science.1167742

Lee, R.M., 1993. *Doing research on sensitive topics.* Sage Publications.

Leonelli, S., 2018b. *La ricerca scientifica nell'era dei big data: Cinque modi in cui i Big Data danneggiano la scienza, e come salvarla.* Meltemi Editore.

Lewthwaite, S. and Holmes, M. M., 2018. The pedagogy of social science research methods textbooks: A scoping study. *Society for Research in Higher Education.* https://eprints.soton.ac.uk/422903/1/Lewthwaite_Pedagogy_of_Social_Science_Research_Methods_Textbooks.pdf [Accessed 7 June 2024].

Lewthwaite, S. and Nind, M., 2016. Teaching research methods in the social sciences: Expert perspectives on pedagogy and practice. *British Journal of Educational Studies, 64*(4): 1-17. https://doi.org/10.1080/00071005.2016.1197882

Lombi, L., 2015. La ricerca sociale al tempo dei big data: Sfide e prospettive. *Studi di Sociologia,* 2: 215-227.

Longo, M., 2005. Sul racconto in sociologia. Letteratura, senso comune, narrazione sociologica. *Foedus,* 12: 25-46.

Longo, M., 2012. *Il sociologo e i racconti: tra letteratura e narrazioni quotidiane.* Carocci.

Longo, M., 2017. Perché le storie contano: brevi considerazioni sul rapporto tra narrazioni e sociologia. Tracce Urbane. *Rivista Italiana Transdisciplinare di Studi Urbani, 1*(2): 65-81.

Lovekamp, W.E., Soboroff, S.D. and Gillespie, M.D., 2017. Engaging students in survey research projects across research methods and statistics courses. *Teaching Sociology, 45*(1): 65-72. https://doi.org/10.1177/0092055X16673136

Lupton, D. 2020. *Data selves: More-than-human perspectives.* Polity Press.

Lupton, D., 2014. *Digital sociology.* Routledge. https://doi.org/10.4324/9781315776880

Lupton, D., Mewburn, I. and Thomson, P., eds., 2017. *The digital academic: Critical perspectives on digital technologies in higher education.* Routledge.

Lury, C. and Marres, N., 2015. Notes on objectual valuation. In M. Kornberger, L. Justesen, A.K. Madsen and J. Mouritsen, (Eds.), *Making things valuable* (pp. 232-256). Oxford University Press. https://doi.org/10.1093/acprof:oso/9780198712282.003.0012

Ma'arop, A. H. and Embi, M. A., 2016. Implementation of blended learning in higher learning institutions: A review of the literature. *International Education Studies, 9*(3): 41-52. https://doi.org/10.5539/ies.v9n3p41

Maines, D. R., 1993. Narrative's moment and sociology's phenomena: Toward a narrative sociology. *The Sociological Quarterly, 34*(1): 17-38. https://doi.org/10.1111/j.1533-8525.1993.tb00128.x

Markham, A. and Buchanan, E., 2012. Ethical decision-making and Internet research: Recommendations from the AoIR Ethics Working Committee (Version 2.0). *Association of Internet Researchers.* https://aoir.org/reports/ethics2.pdf [Accessed 7 June 2024].

Marradi, A., 1996. Metodo come arte. *Quaderni di sociologia,* 10: 71-92. https://doi.org/10.4000/qds.6358

Marradi, A., 2005. *Raccontar storie. Un nuovo metodo per indagare sui valori.* Carocci.

Marradi, A., 2007. *Metodologia delle scienze sociali.* Il Mulino.

Marres, N., 2012. The redistribution of methods: On intervention in digital social research, broadly conceived. *The Sociological Review,* 60: 139-165. https://doi.org/10.1111/j.1467-954X.2012.02121.x

Marres, N., 2017. *Digital sociology: The reinvention of social research.* John Wiley and Sons.

Marres, N. and Weltevrede, E., 2013. Scraping the social? Issues in live social research. *Journal of Cultural Economy,* 6(3): 313-335. https://doi.org/10.10 80/17530350.2013.772070

Marzano, A., 2012. L'organizzazione universitaria: Una ricerca sulla percezione degli studenti. *Giornale Italiano della Ricerca Educativa,* V: 130-144.

Mattar, J., Souza, Á. L. M. and de Oliveira Beduschi, J., 2017. Games para o ensino de metodologia científica: Revisão de literatura e boas práticas. *Educação, Formação and Tecnologias,* 10(1): 3-19.

Melucci, A., 1996. *Challenging codes: Collective action in the information age.* Cambridge University Press. https://doi.org/10.1017/CBO9780511520891

Memoli, R., 2004. *Strategie e strumenti della ricerca sociale.* Franco Angeli.

Memoli, R., 2009. La formazione metodologica nelle lauree magistrali. In A. Baldissera, (Ed.), Insegnare metodologia delle scienze sociali (pp. 207-215). Bonanno.

Menichetti, L., 2017. Tecnologie come oggetto di apprendimento: Come sviluppare competenze digitali. In G. Bonaiuti, A. Calvani, L. Menichetti and G. Vivanet, (Eds.), Le tecnologie educative (pp. 125-178). Carocci.

Meraviglia, C., 2004. *Metodologia delle scienze sociali: Un'introduzione.* Carocci.

Messina, L. and De Rossi, M., (Eds.), 2015. *Tecnologie, formazione e didattica.* Carocci.

Messina, L., and Tabone, S., 2014. Technology in university teaching: An exploratory research into TPACK, proficiency, and beliefs of Education faculty. *Cadmo,* 22(1): 89-110. https://doi.org/10.3280/CAD2014-001009

Milani, M., Raffaghelli, J. E., and Ghislandi, P. M. M., 2017. Fuori orario. Il tempo docente nella didattica online. *Italian Journal of Educational Technology,* 25(3): 35-54.

Mingo, I., 2009. *Concetti e quantità: Percorsi di statistica sociale.* Bonanno.

Mishler, E. G., 1986. *Research Interviewing: context and narrative.* Harvard University Press. https://doi.org/10.4159/9780674041141

Mishler, E. G., 1995. Models of narrative analysis: a typology. *Journal of Narrative and Life History,* 5(2): 87-123. https://doi.org/10.1075/jnlh.5.2.01mod

Mishra, P., and Koehler, M. J., 2006. Technological pedagogical content knowledge: A framework for teacher knowledge. *Teachers college record,* 108(6): 1017. https://doi.org/10.1177/016146810610800610

Mittelstadt, B. 2019. Principles alone cannot guarantee ethical AI. *Nature machine intelligence,* 1(11): 501-507. https://doi.org/10.1038/s42256-019-0114-4

Molina, M. and Garip, F., 2019. Machine learning for sociology. *Annual Review of Sociology,* 45: 27-45. https://doi.org/10.1146/annurev-soc-073117-041106

Montesperelli, P., 1998. *L'intervista ermeneutica*. FrancoAngeli.

Murtonen, M., 2015. University students' understanding of the concepts empirical, theoretical, qualitative and quantitative research. *Teaching in Higher Education, 20*(7): 684-698. https://doi.org/10.1080/13562517.2015.1072152

Murtonen, M. and Lehtinen, E., 2003. Difficulties experienced by education and sociology students in quantitative methods courses. *Studies in Higher Education, 28*(2): 171-185. https://doi.org/10.1080/0307507032000058064

Nedeva, V., 2005. The possibilities of e-learning, based on Moodle software platform. *Trakia Journal of Sciences, 3*(7): 12-19.

Neresini, F., 2017. On data, big data and social research: Is it really a revolution? In: N.C. Lauro, E. Amaturo, M.G. Grassia, B. Aragona, and M. Marino, (Eds.), *Data science and social research: Epistemology, methods, technology and applications* (pp. 9-16). Springer International.

Ni, A. Y., 2013. Comparing the effectiveness of classroom and online learning: Teaching research methods. *Journal of Public Affairs Education, 19*(2): 199-215. https://doi.org/10.1080/15236803.2013.12001730

Nind, M., Kilburn, D. and Luff, R., 2015. The teaching and learning of social research methods: Developments in pedagogical knowledge. *International Journal of Social Research Methodology, 18*(5): 545-561. https://doi.org/10.1080/13645579.2015.1062631

Nind, M. and Lewthwaite, S., 2020. A conceptual-empirical typology of social science research methods pedagogy. *Research Papers in Education, 35*(4): 467-487. https://doi.org/10.1080/02671522.2019.1601756

Nind, M. M., Holmes, M., Insenga, M., Lewthwaite, S. and Sutton, C., 2019. Student perspectives on learning research methods in the social sciences. *Teaching in Higher Education* (pp. 1-15). https://doi.org/10.1080/13562517.2019.1592150

Njenga, J. K. and Fourie, L. C. H., 2010. The myths about e-learning in higher education. *British Journal of Educational Technology, 41*(2): 199-212. https://doi.org/10.1111/j.1467-8535.2008.00910.x

Nolan, D. and Perrett, J., 2016. Teaching and Learning Data Visualisation: Ideas and Assignments, *The American Statistician, 70*(3): 260-269. https://doi.org/10.1080/00031305.2015.1123651

Padovani, C., Pavan, E. and Cernison, M., 2009. Appendice. Che cos' è e come funziona Issue Crawler. *Quaderni di Sociologia, 49*: 81-88. https://doi.org/10.4000/qds.807

Palfrey, J. and Gasser, U., 2008. Opening universities in a digital era. *New England Journal of Higher Education, 23*(1): 22-24.

Pandolfini, V., 2016. Exploring the impact of ICTs in education: Controversies and challenges. *Italian Journal of Sociology of Education, 8*(2): 28-53. https://doi.org/10.14658/pupj-ijse-2016-2-3.

Papanastasiou, E.C., 2005. Factor structure of the attitudes toward research scale. *Statistics Education Research Journal, 4*(1): 16-26. https://doi.org/10.52041/serj.v4i1.523

Papanastasiou, E. C. and Zembylas, M., 2008. Anxiety in undergraduate research methods courses: Its nature and implications. *International Journal of Research and Method in Education*, *31*(2): 155-167. https://doi.org/10.10 80/17437270802124616

Payne, G. and Williams, M., 2011. *Teaching quantitative methods: Getting the basics right.* Sage. https://doi.org/10.4135/9781446268384

Pecchinenda, G., 2009. *La narrazione della società. Appunti introduttivi alla sociologia dei processi culturali e comunicativi.* Ipermedium.

Peirce, C.S., 1998. On the Logic of Drawing History from Ancient Documents. In Peirce Edition Project (Ed.), *The Essential Peirce: Selected Philosophical Writings, 1893–1913* (pp. 85-115), II. Indiana University Press.

Perelman, C. and Olbrechts-Tyteca, L., 1969. *The new rhetoric: a treatise on argumentation.* Translated by J. Wilkinson and P. Weaver. University of Notre Dame Press.

Pfeffer, C. A. and Rogalin, C. L., 2012. Three strategies for teaching research methods: A case study. *Teaching Sociology*, *40*(4): 368-376. https://doi.org/10.1177/0092055X12446783

Pink, S. 2022. Methods for researching automated futures. *Qualitative Inquiry*, *28*(7): 747-753. https://doi.org/10.1177/10778004221096845

Pitrone, M. C., 2009. *Sondaggi e interviste. Lo studio dell'opinione pubblica nella ricerca sociale.* Milano: Franco Angeli.

Polkinghorne, D. E., 1988. *Narrative knowing and the human sciences.* State University of New York Press.

Poggio, B., 2004. *Mi racconti una storia. Il metodo narrativo nelle scienze sociali.* Carocci.

Pompili, G., and Viterritti, A. (2018). Between Experimentation and Accountability: Challenges for Academic Teaching Innovation. *Abstract of 7th Ethnography and qualitative research conference* (p. 34).

Radha, R., Mahalakshmi, K., Sathis Kumar, V. and Saravanakumar, A. R., 2020. E-learning during lockdown of COVID-19 pandemic: A global perspective. *International Journal of Control and Automation*, *13*(4): 1088-1099.

Ranieri, M., 2005. *Strategie e strumenti della ricerca sociale.* Franco Angeli.

Ranieri, M., 2011. *Le insidie dell'ovvio: Tecnologie educative e critica della retorica tecno-centrica.* ETS.

Ranieri, M., Raffaghelli, J. E., and Pezzati, F., 2018. Digital resources for faculty development in e-learning: a self-paced approach for professional learning. *Italian Journal of Educational Technology*, *26*(1): 104-118.

Rapanta, C., Botturi, L., Goodyear, P., Guàrdia, L. and Koole, M., 2020. Online university teaching during and after the COVID-19 crisis: Refocusing teacher presence and learning activity. *Postdigital Science and Education*. https://doi.org/10.1007/s42438-020-00155-y

Reilly, J. M., Ring, J. and Duke, L., 2005. Visual thinking strategies: A new role for art in medical education. *Family Medicine*, *37*(4): 250-252.

Rennie, F., and Morrison, T., 2013. *E-learning and social networking handbook: Resources for higher education.* Routledge. https://doi.org/10.4324/97802031 20279

Renzi, S., Klobas, J., and Trentin, G., 2008. Come favorire l'avvicinamento dei docenti universitari all'uso didattico delle ICT. In *Didamatica. Annual Conference of AICA.* Laterza.

Rieder, B., 2013. Studying Facebook via data extraction: The Netvizz application. In *Proceedings of the 5th Annual ACM Web Science Conference* (pp. 346-355). Association for Computing Machinery. https://doi.org/10.1145/2464464.2464475

Rienties, B., Brouwer, N., and Lygo-Baker, S., 2013. The effects of online professional development on higher education teachers' beliefs and intentions towards learning facilitation and technology. *Teaching and teacher education,* 29: 122-131. https://doi.org/10.1016/j.tate.2012.09.002

Riessman, C. K., 1993. *Doing narrative analysis.* Sage Publications.

Riessman, C. K., 2008. *Narrative methods for the human sciences.* Sage.

Risi, E., 2022. *Vite datificate. Modelli di ricerca nella società delle piattaforme.* Franco Angeli.

Roberts, S., Snee, H., Hine, C., Morey, Y. and Watson, H., (Eds.), 2016. *Digital methods for social science: An interdisciplinary guide to research innovation.* Palgrave Macmillan.

Robinson, K. M., 2001. Unsolicited narratives from the Internet: a rich source of qualitative data. *Qualitative health research, 11*(5): 706-714. https://doi.org/10.1177/104973201129119398

Rock, A. J., Coventry, W. L., Morgan, M. I. and Loi, N. M., 2016. Teaching research methods and statistics in e-learning environments: Pedagogy, practical examples, and possible futures. *Frontiers in Psychology,* 7: 339. https://doi.org/10.3389/fpsyg.2016.00339

Rogers, R., 2009. *The end of the virtual: Digital methods.* Amsterdam University Press. https://doi.org/10.5117/9789056295936

Rogers, R., 2013. *Digital methods.* MIT Press. https://doi.org/10.7551/mitpress/8718.001.0001

Rogers, R., 2015. Digital methods for web research. In R. Scott, and S. Kosslyn, (Eds.), *Emerging trends in the social and behavioral sciences: An interdisciplinary, searchable, and linkable resource* (pp. 1-22). John Wiley and Sons. https://doi.org/10.1002/9781118900772.etrds0076

Rogers, R., and Lewthwaite, S., 2019. Teaching Digital Methods: Interview with Richard Rogers. Interviewer: S. Lewthwaite. *Diseña,* 14: 12-37. https://doi.org/10.7764/disena.14.12-37

Romney, M., Johnson, R. G. and Roschke, K., 2017. Narratives of life experience in the digital space: a case study of the images in Richard Deitsch's single best moment project. *Information, Communication and Society, 20*(7): 1040-1056. https://doi.org/10.1080/1369118X.2016.1203976

Rosenberg, 2001. *E-learning: strategies for delivering knowledge in the digital age.* McGraw-Hill Professional.

Rossi, P. G., 2010. *Tecnologia e costruzione di mondi: post-costruttivismo, linguaggi e ambienti di apprendimento.* Armando editore.

Roulston, K., 2010. *Reflective interviewing: A guide to theory and practice.* Sage. https://doi.org/10.4135/9781446288009

Ruijer, E., Grimmelikhuijsen, S., van den Berg, J., and Meijer, A., 2020. Open data work: understanding open data usage from a practice lens. *International Review of Administrative Sciences, 86*(1): 3-19. https://doi.org/10.1177/0020852317753068

Ryan, L., Silver, D., Laramee, R. S., and Ebert, D., 2019. Teaching data visualisation as a skill. *IEEE Computer Graphics and Applications, 39*(2): 95-103. https://doi.org/10.1109/MCG.2018.2889526

Sacchetti, F., 2012. Abduzione e scoperta nella ricerca sociale. *Studi di Sociologia:* 403-427.

Salavati, S., 2017. Dilemmas in Teachers' Use of Digital Technologies in Everyday School Practice. In *Dilemmas 2015. Papers from the 18th Annual International Conference Dilemmas for Human Services: Organizing, Designing and Managing* (pp. 1-11). Linnaeus University.

Sandrini, M., and Colombo, M., 2008. E-learning prospettiva sociologica. In M. Colombo, *E-learning e cambiamenti sociali. Dal competere al comprendere* (pp. 1-17). Liguori.

Sangrà, A., Vlachopoulos, D. and Cabrera, N., 2012. Building an inclusive definition of e-learning: An approach to the conceptual framework. *The International Review of Research in Open and Distributed Learning, 13*(2): 145-159. https://doi.org/10.19173/irrodl.v13i2.1161

Savage, M. and Burrows, R., 2007. The coming crisis of empirical sociology. *Sociology, 41*(5): 885-899. https://doi.org/10.1177/0038038507080443

Schön, D.A., 1983. *The reflective practitioner: How professionals think in action.* Basic Books.

Schön, D.A., 1987. *Educating the reflective practitioner: Toward a new design for teaching and learning in the professions.* Jossey-Bass.

Schütz, A., 1967. *The phenomenology of the social world.* Northwestern University Press.

Seale, C., Charteris-Black, J., MacFarlane, A. and McPherson, A., 2010. Interviews and internet forums: a comparison of two sources of qualitative data. *Qualitative Health Research, 20*(5): 595-606. https://doi.org/10.1177/1049732309354094

Selwyn, N., 2019. *What is digital sociology?* John Wiley & Sons.

Sillaots, M., 2014. Achieving flow through gamification: A study on re-designing research methods courses. In: C. Busch, (Ed.), *VIII European Conference on Games Based Learning* (pp. 538-545). Academic Conferences International Limited.

Silverman, D. (Ed.), 2016. *Qualitative research.* Sage.

Shulman, L., 1987. Knowledge and teaching: Foundations of the new reform. *Harvard Educational Review, 57*(1): 1-23. https://doi.org/10.17763/haer.57.1.j463w79r56455411

Snee, H., Hine, C., Morey, Y., Roberts, S. and Watson, H., (Eds.), 2016. *Digital methods for social science: An interdisciplinary guide to research innovation.* Springer. https://doi.org/10.1057/9781137453662

Snelson, C., Wertz, C. I., Onstott, K., and Bader, J., 2017. Using World of Warcraft to teach research methods in online doctoral education: A student-instructor duoethnography. *The Qualitative Report, 22*(5): 1439-1456. https://doi.org/10.46743/2160-3715/2017.2709

Snelson, C., 2019. Teaching qualitative research methods online: A scoping review of the literature. *The Qualitative Report, 24*(11): 2799-2814. https://doi.org/10.46743/2160-3715/2019.4021

Somers, M. R., 1994. The narrative constitution of identity: A relational and network approach. *Theory and society,* *23*(5): 605-649. https://doi.org/10.10 07/BF00992905

Stefanizzi, S., 2012. *Il ragionamento sociologico: Questioni metodologiche ed esempi di ricerca.* McGraw-Hill.

Stone, E., Gabard, A., Groves, A. and Lipkus, I., 2015. Effects of Numerical Versus Foreground- Only Icon Displays on Understanding of Risk Magnitudes. *Journal of health communication,* 20: 1-12. https://doi.org/10.1080/108107 30.2015.1018594

Strangman, L. and Knowles, E., 2012. Improving the development of students' research questions and hypotheses in an introductory business research methods course. *International Journal for the Scholarship of Teaching and Learning,* *6*(2). https://digitalcommons.georgiasouthern.edu/ij-sotl/vol6/iss2/ 24/ [Accessed 7 June 2024]. https://doi.org/10.20429/ijsotl.2012.060224

Tamim, R. M., Bernard, R. M., Borokhovski, E., Abrami, P. C. and Schmid, R. F., 2011. What forty years of research says about the impact of technology on learning: A second-order meta-analysis and validation study. *Review of Educational Research,* *81*(1): 4-28. https://doi.org/10.3102/0034654310393361

Tammaro, R., Petolicchio, A. and D'Alessio, A., 2017. Formazione dei docenti e sistemi di reclutamento: un leitmotiv, *Giornale italiano della ricerca educativa,* 19: 54-67.

Tarifa, F. and Zhupa, A., 2014. Theory, imagination, and practice: Teaching sociological theory at the university. *Journal of the World Universities Forum,* *7*(1): 33-43. https://doi.org/10.18848/1835-2030/CGP/v07i01/56843

Taylor, J. C., 2002. Teaching and learning online: The workers, the lurkers and the shirkers. In *Proceedings of the 2nd Conference on Research in Distance and Adult Learning in Asia* (p. 31). Open University of Hong Kong.

Thompson, C. J., Leonard, L. and Bridier, N., 2019. Online discussion forums: Quality interactions for reducing statistics anxiety in graduate education students. *International Journal of E-Learning and Distance Education,* *34*(1): 1-31.

Thomas, W. I. and Znaniecki, F., 1984. *The polish peasant in Europe and America.* University of Illinois Press. https://doi.org/10.2307/25140618

Thumim, N., 2009. 'Everyone has a story to tell' Mediation and self-representation in two UK institutions. *International Journal of Cultural Studies,* *12*(6): 617-638. https://doi.org/10.1177/1367877909342494

Tonegato, P., 2006. Lavorare a distanza. In E. Felisatti, *Cooperare in team e in classe* (pp. 87-102). Pensa Multimedia.

Trentin, G., 2003. Gestire la complessità dei sistemi di e-learning. *Atti del convegno annuale Didamatica:* 1-8.

Trentin, G., 2006. Tecnology Enhanced Learning e didattica universitaria: i diversi approcci e i motivi della loro scelta. *TD-Tecnologie Didattiche,* 37: 3-9.

Trowler, P. R., 2005. A sociology of teaching, learning and enhancement: Improving practices in higher education. *Revista de Sociologia,* 76: 13-32. https://doi.org/10.5565/rev/papers/v76n0.969

Tufte, E.R., 1990. *Envisioning information.* Graphics Press.

Tusini, S., 2006. *La ricerca come relazione: l'intervista nelle scienze sociali.* Franco Angeli.

Urh, M., Vukovic, G., Jereb, E. and Pintar, R., 2015. The model for introduction of gamification into e-learning in higher education. *Procedia - Social and Behavioral Sciences, 197*(25): 388-397. https://doi.org/10.1016/j.sbspro.2015. 07.154

Van Atteveldt, W. and Peng, T.Q., 2018. When communication meets computation: Opportunities, challenges, and pitfalls in computational communication science. *Communication Methods and Measures, 12*(2-3): 81-92. https://doi.org/10. 1080/19312458.2018.1458084

Veltri, G.A., 2019. *Digital social research.* John Wiley & Sons.

Vidotto Fonda, G., 2016. *Le mappe dei concetti nella ricerca sociale.* Franco Angeli.

Wakeford, J., 1981. From methods to practice: A critical note on the teaching of research practice to undergraduates. *Sociology, 15*(4): 505-512. https://doi. org/10.1177/003803858101500404

Wagner, C., Garner, M. and Kawulich, B., 2011. The state of the art of teaching research methods in the social sciences: Towards a pedagogical culture. *Studies in Higher Education, 36*(1): 75-92. https://doi.org/10.1080/030750709 03452594

Webb, M. and Cox, M., 2004. A review of pedagogy related to information and communications technology. *Technology, Pedagogy and Education, 13*(3): 235-286. https://doi.org/10.1080/14759390400200183

Wenger, E., 1999. *Communities of practice: Learning, meaning, and identity.* Cambridge University Press. https://doi.org/10.1017/CBO9780511803932

Wickham, H. and Grolemund, G., 2016. *R for Data Science.* O'Reilly Media.

Williams, M., Payne, G., Hodgkinson, L. and Poade, D., 2008. Does British sociology count? Sociology students' attitudes toward quantitative methods. *Sociology, 42*(5): 1003-1021. https://doi.org/10.1177/0038038508094576

Williamson, B., Bayne, S. and Shay, S., 2020. The datafication of teaching in higher education: Critical issues and perspectives. *Teaching in Higher Education, 25*(4): 351-365. https://doi.org/10.1080/13562517.2020.1748811

Wills, T., 2016. Social media as a research method. *Communication Research and Practice, 2*(1): 7-19. https://doi.org/10.1080/22041451.2016.1155312

Winn, S., 1995. Learning by doing: Teaching research methods through student participation in a commissioned research project. *Studies in Higher Education, 20*(2): 203-214. https://doi.org/10.1080/03075079512331381703

Wolfe, J., 2015. Teaching students to focus on the data in data visualisation. *Journal of Business and Technical Communication, 29*(3): 344-359. https:// doi.org/10.1177/1050651915573944

Yip, M.C.W., 2004. Using WebCT to teach courses online. *British Journal of Educational Technology, 35*(4): 497-501. https://doi.org/10.1111/j.0007-1013. 2004.00407.x

Zhang, Y., 2018. Converging data storytelling and visualisation. In E. Clua, L. Roque, A. Lugmayr and P. Tuomi, (Eds.), *Entertainment Computing – ICEC 2018* (pp. 310-316). Springer. https://doi.org/10.1007/978-3-319-99426-0_36

Zhu, C., 2011. Teacher roles and adoption of educational technology in the Chinese context. *Journal for Educational Research Online/Journal für Bildungsforschung Online, 2*(2): 72-86.

Ziewitz, M. 2016. Governing algorithms: Myth, mess, and methods. *Science, Technology, & Human Values, 41*(1): 3-16. https://doi.org/10.1177/016224391 5608948

Zimmer, M. and Kinder-Kurlanda, K., (Eds.), 2017. *Internet Research Ethics for the Social Age: New Challenges, Cases, and Contexts.* Peter Lang. https://doi.org/10.3726/b11077

Zuckerman, O., Gal-Oz, A., Peretz, O., Weisberg, O. and Tarrasch, R., 2015. Leveraging mobile technology to engage college students in scientific research. In *Proceedings of the 17th International Conference on Human-Computer Interaction with Mobile Devices and Services* (pp. 470-477). Association for Computing Machinery. https://doi.org/10.1145/2785830.2785870

Zywica, J. and Danowski, J., 2008. The faces of Facebookers: Investigating social enhancement and social compensation hypotheses; predicting Facebook™ and offline popularity from sociability and self esteem, and mapping the meanings of popularity with semantic networks. *Journal of Computer-Mediated Communication, 14*(1): 1-34. https://doi.org/10.1111/j.1083-6101.2008.01429.x

Appendix:
Figures and Tables

Appendix Introduction

This appendix collects a series of figures and tables developed by students during their final group projects in the Social Research Methods courses at the University of Salerno. These projects are a concrete outcome of the pedagogical approach discussed throughout the book, which emphasises the integration of digital tools into methodological training and the active involvement of students in applied research activities.

The included figures illustrate different forms of data visualisation, ranging from basic statistical representations to more complex visual formats such as tree maps, word clouds, and thematic cartography. They demonstrate the students' ability to use digital platforms such as Tableau Public, WordArt, and other visualisation tools to organise, analyse, and present data meaningfully. In parallel, the tables provide a structured synthesis of the students' research work, summarizing key methodological features and patterns emerging from their analyses.

This appendix is not intended merely as a repository of student work. Rather, it serves a dual purpose: First, it highlights how the adoption of digital technologies fosters new skills in interpreting and presenting social data, promoting critical thinking, visual literacy, and collaborative knowledge production among students. Second, it provides evidence of how a redefined pedagogical model – based on blended learning, digital experimentation, and hands-on engagement – can transform traditional teaching practices in social research methods.

Each project involved a complete research cycle, including the formulation of research questions, data collection (often from online or secondary digital sources), data analysis, and the production of original visualisations. Students were encouraged to explore contemporary social phenomena through an empirical lens while critically reflecting on methodological choices, limitations, and interpretative frameworks.

The materials presented here were selected to showcase the diversity of topics addressed by the students – from political protest movements to digital sports fandom – as well as the variety of techniques and creativity displayed in presenting research results. They also underline some of the challenges discussed in the main chapters of the book: the epistemological reconfiguration of research methods in the digital era, the democratization of data analysis tools, and the centrality of visualisation in constructing and communicating sociological knowledge.

In order to maintain consistency with academic standards, the figures and tables in this appendix are numbered following the format prescribed for appendices (A.1, A.2, etc.). A brief caption accompanies each item to contextualize its content and specify the source and processing method where relevant. It is important to note that while many of the datasets used were derived from publicly available sources, some visualisations based on external platforms may include materials subject to copyright; in those cases, students worked within the permitted frameworks of educational and research use.

By making this appendix available, the intention is to offer readers a tangible view of how theoretical reflection, methodological rigor, and digital innovation can converge in university teaching practices, preparing students not only to master social research methods but also to critically engage with the digital transformation of contemporary society.

Figure A.1. Comparison of areas in Iran where major protests occurred. Intensity of protest incidents. Source: Processed with Tableau Public. Final Project Group A - Iran Case.

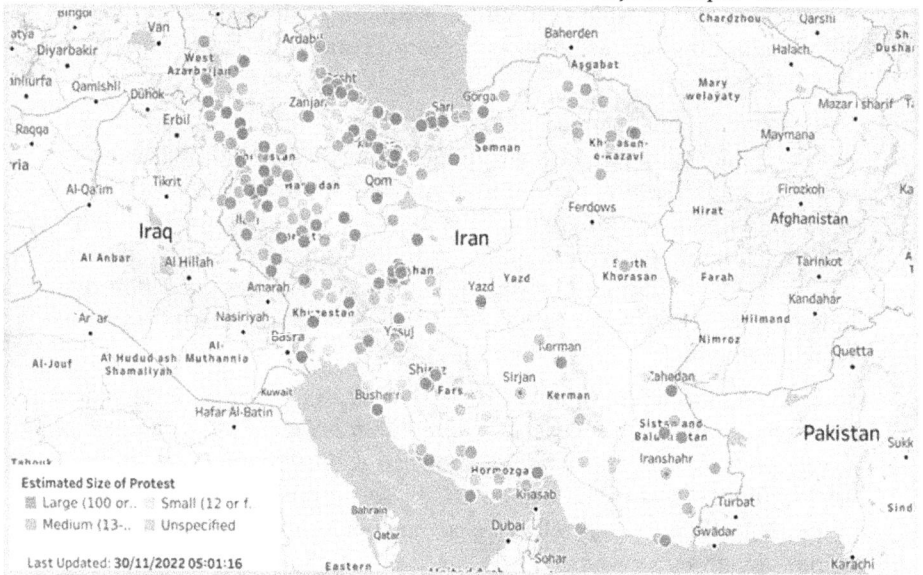

Figure A.2. Most discussed topics on Facebook and Instagram. Final Project Group E - Farfalle Case. Processed with Tableau.

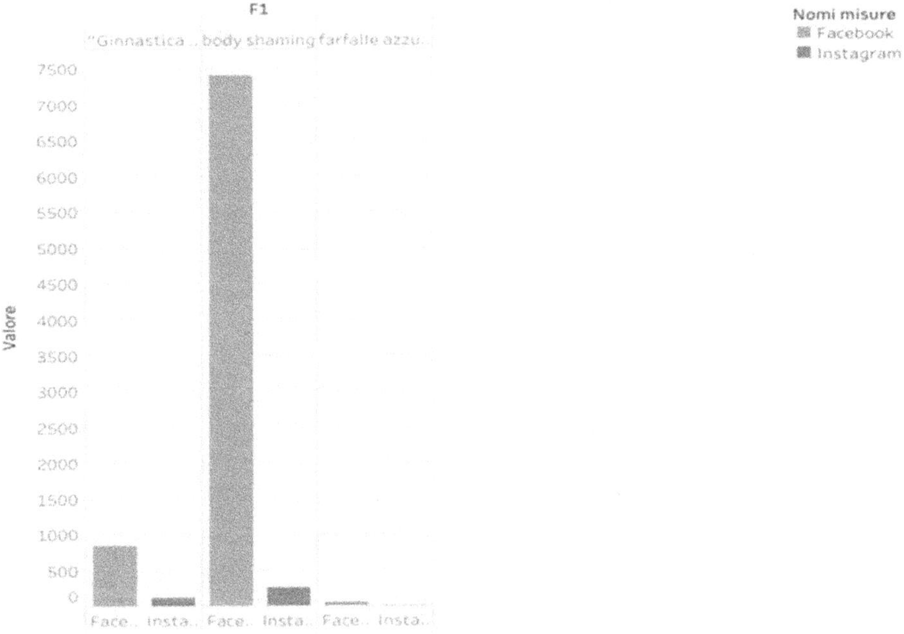

Figure A.3. Word Cloud - Data Source: Blogmeter - Data Processing: Word Art. Final Project Group B - Egonu Case.

Figure A.4. Growth of Followers on Paola Egonu's Instagram Profile. Final Project of Group B.

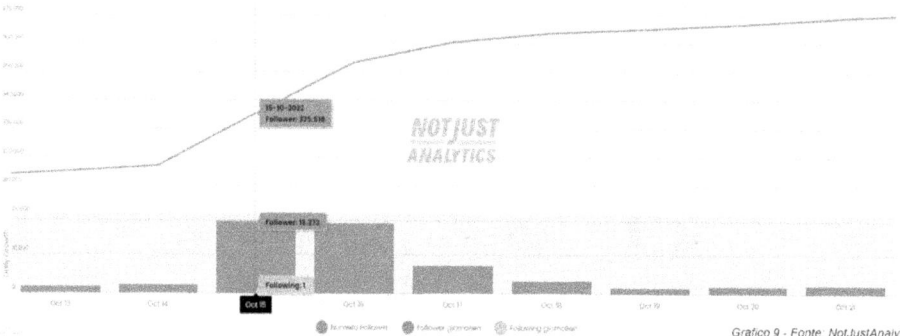

CRESCITA DI FOLLOWER SU INSTAGRAM
Periodo di riferimento: dal 13 ottobre al 20 ottobre

15 ottobre	16 ottobre
+18.373	+17.876

Grafico 9 - Fonte: NotJustAnalytics

Figure A.5. Italians' Mood Regarding the World Cup. Final Project of Group D.
Processed with Tableau.

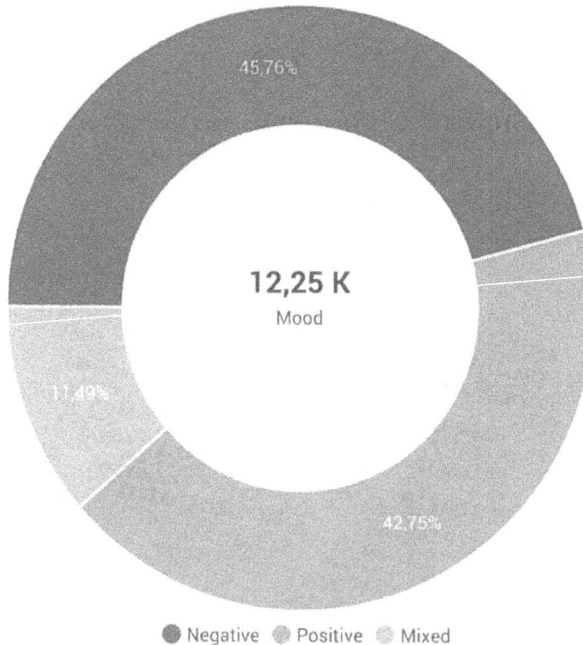

Figure A.6. The Tree Map Shows the Italian Universities with the Highest Number of Followers on LinkedIn. Final Project of Group F. Processed with Tableau.

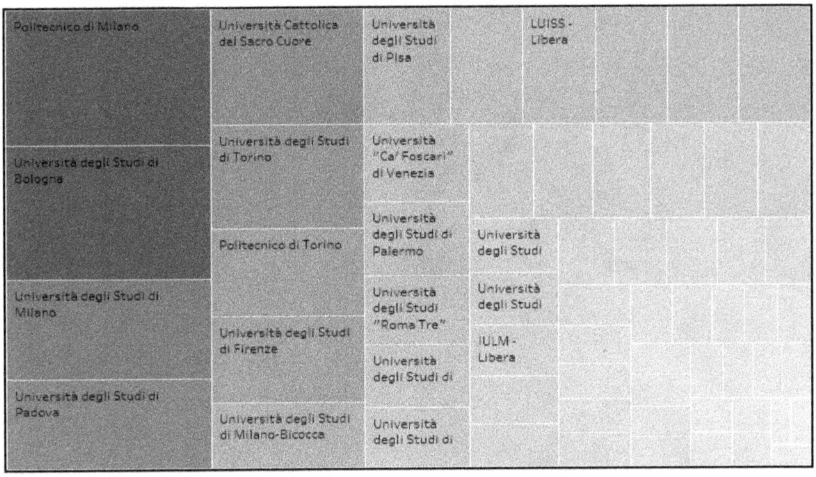

Figure A.7. Frequency of the Word 'Paralympics' on Social Media (January-December 2022). Final Project of Group C. Processed with Tableau.

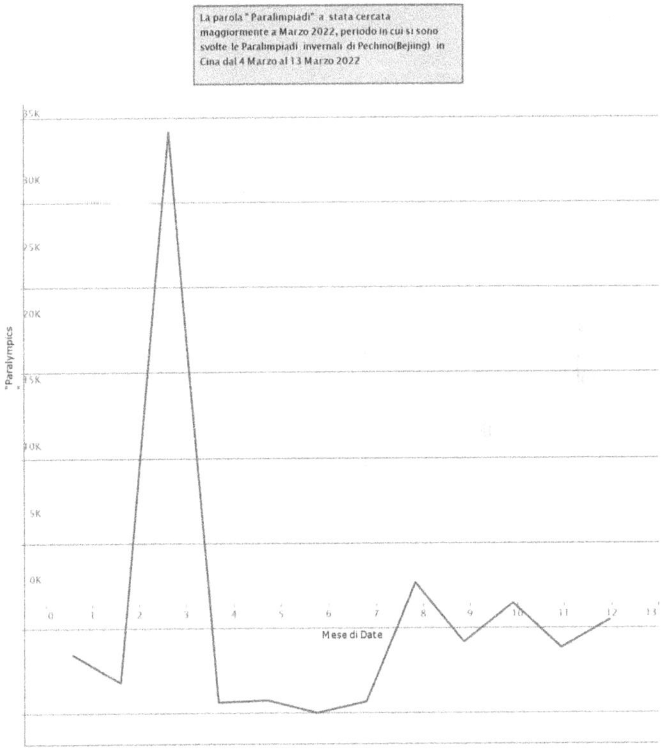

Figure A.8. The map chart shows the 'volume of mentions' by the number of searches for the keyword 'Paola Egonu' by region in Italy between October 13 and 20, 2022. Final Project of Group B. Processed with Tableau.

Regioni		Regioni	
Valle d'Aosta	100	Valle d'Aosta	100
Sardegna	81	Sardegna	81
Liguria	72	Liguria	72
Veneto	64	Veneto	64
Friuli-Venezia Giulia	64	Friuli-Venezia Giulia	64
Piemonte	62	Piemonte	62
Emilia-Romagna	60	Emilia-Romagna	60
Toscana	59	Toscana	59
Abruzzo	59	Abruzzo	59
Trentino-Alto Adige	57	Trentino-Alto Adige	57
Marche	54	Marche	54
Lombardia	54	Lombardia	54
Lazio	49	Lazio	49
Basilicata	40	Basilicata	40
Calabria	39	Calabria	39
Umbria	38	Umbria	38
Campania	38	Campania	38
Puglia	37	Puglia	37
Sicilia	26	Sicilia	26
Molise	1	Molise	1

Index